Becoming Better Business Leaders

Book 1

How Smart Leaders Build Stronger Teams and Organizations

The No-Name Mastermind Group

Albert B. Blixt, Jeffrey Edwards,
Dr. Mike Hackney, Robert Grossman,
& Ski Swiatkowski

Becoming Better Business Leaders
Volume 1 - How Smart Leaders Build
Stronger Teams and Organizations

ISBN-13: 978-1957328560

Published by Sordelet Ink
www.sordeletink.com

Becoming Better Business Leaders

Book 1
How Smart Leaders Build Stronger Teams and Organizations

The No-Name Mastermind Group

Albert B. Blixt, Jeffrey Edwards,
Dr. Mike Hackney, Robert Grossman,
& Ski Swiatkowski

SORDELET ink

CONTENTS

Forward—and Forward!

Welcome to Volume One of the extended learnings of the No-Name Mastermind Group, a collection of business consultants from a variety of business areas, backgrounds, and cultures in North America.

This is a continuing series by the authors on a variety of business and business leadership topics. Coming books will have additional 'visiting consultants' providing their perspectives to the collective wisdom—or lack thereof—of the core group of No-Name members,

The topics of this eclectic band range across the board from all facets of business operating areas and entrepreneurship. While we do not do taxes, recommend financial strategies or give legal or medical advice, our own craziness will not stop us from offering opinions on yours.

Our goal is not to write literature—Shakespeare can be found on Amazon if desired! Rather our goal is sharing our experiences and those of our anonymous clients to assist you in seeing viewpoints that may assist with similar issues on your own plate. Also, each of us is available within our areas of focus if you'd like to reach out for specific consulting inquiries or engagements.

Join us on our weekly YouTube program where Robert Grossman will interview a chapter author on their latest contribution, the background of the chapter, and other lessons learned from that and similar events. As each new book is published, the following ten weeks on the program will delve weekly into one of the respective chapters.

We welcome your feedback! Are there topics you'd like us to address in subsequent editions? We'll move forward with Book Two in another three months or so, but subsequent books are always in some degree of development until they are locked in about three months prior to publication.

Please address your comments to:

thenonamemastermind@gmail.com

Becoming Better Business Leaders

Chapter One

Launching a Team-based Renewal Effort Using Whole-Scale Methodology: The Ferranti-Packard Story

By Albert B. Blixt

(Author's note: While this story takes place many years ago, the lessons remain true today)

Introduction

In less than one year, Ferranti-Packard Transformers, a troubled Ontario, Canada manufacturing plant, achieved a remarkable turnaround by involving its employees in both formulating and implementing a new strategic plan for the business. The process relied heavily on the use of teams, including worker participation in a two-day *Whole-Scale*™ change event using the "one-brain, one-heart" methods of Dannemiller Tyson Associates. Results have included: an empowered workforce, improved labor management relations and increases in quality, productivity and profitability.

The purpose of this chapter is to detail how whole-system change methodology makes use of teams and how the people of one plant became engaged in creating fast and far-reaching change in their plant. It is written from my perspective as of one of the consultants who participated in the change process.

Business Situation: Ferranti-Packard Transformers, Ltd.

Ferranti-Packard Transformers, Ltd. manufactures power transformers for public utilities and industrial clients in three plants located in Ontario, Quebec and Mexico. It is a division of Rolls-Royce of Canada, Ltd. which, in turn, is part of Rolls-Royce of the United Kingdom.

In the fall of 1995, the outlook for the Ferranti-Packard plant at St. Catharines, Ontario was bleak. With sales revenues of approximately $40 million, the plant had lost money for several years and was on track to lose $4.5 million in 1995. Plagued by a flat market, tough competition, high quality costs (rework), delivery problems and an adversarial labor-management climate, the St. Catharines plant was in trouble with its customers, its workers and its owners in Toronto and London. New leadership was clearly needed.

In August 1995, Pierre Racine became the head all Ferranti-Packard operations. He took personal charge of the operations at St. Catharines. He was the fourth CEO in three years. Racine's job was to turn the plant around "soon" or it would be closed or sold. "Rolls-Royce" said, 'This is your last chance, boys. Get it right this time.'" recalls Human Resources VP Scott Smith, who had been on the job only two months when Racine arrived. What they found was a management "team" that wasn't a team at all. They did not meet regularly or communicate effectively. What passed for a strategic plan had been locked in the desk drawer of the previous CEO. There was no shared business plan and no functional strategy for any of the operating functions such as engineering, operations or sales & marketing. There was a surprising lack of knowledge of the marketplace. According to Smith, "There was no clear idea of who our customer was or what they wanted."

Pierre engaged Doug Emerson and his firm, Managerial Design of Oakville, Ontario, to work with him on developing the leadership team. While dealing with the daily crises caused by quality problems, late deliveries and unhappy customers, Racine made time to meet with his six direct reports on almost a weekly basis. He and the group began to work as a team. They developed a draft strategy to turn the business around. By early 1996 they had identified six key result areas that were to be the focus of the strategy.

The Need for a Whole System Intervention

As the strategy took shape, the leadership team recognized that the strategic plan would need the full support of the plant's unions and employees if it was to have any chance of succeeding. That did not appear to likely. Relations with the three locals of the United Steel Workers were not good. Previous management had left an atmosphere of mistrust, cynicism and downright hostility. There was no meaningful communication between management and the union leadership. A way had to be found to unite management, the unions and workers in developing and implementing the new strategy.

In March, 1996, Dannemiller Tyson Associates was contacted to discuss using its *Whole-Scale* methodology to involve all of the internal stakeholders in both strategic planning and rapid implementation. Kathleen Dannemiller and I drove through a snow storm to the plant just outside of Niagara Falls to meet with Pierre and Scott. When we arrived, Pierre was in the midst of conducting a series of informational meetings with workers to share business and financial information that had never been shared before.

We sat in on one of those meetings and simultaneously learned about the business problems and experienced the skepticism and anxiety of the workers. The facts Pierre presented were sobering but his style was open and honest. He answered every tough question candidly. Still, the doubt on the faces of those people leaving the meeting was unmistakable. They had seen too many new leaders and heard too many hopeful scenarios to be convinced by words. They would need to see real action on the part of management before they would support anything.

Kathie Dannemiller and I met with Pierre and Scott Smith after that session. It was decided to close the plant and take everyone off site for a two-day meeting that would bring about the rapid, plant-wide change needed. The event would be designed and facilitated using the *Whole-Scale* methodology. June 13 and 14 were chosen as the dates for the event.

Dannemiller Tyson Associates and Whole-Scale Methodology

Dannemiller Tyson Associates (DTA) was founded in the early 1980's by Kathleen D. Dannemiller and the late Charles Tyson to help organizations achieve fast, long-lasting change. The earliest work was with the Ford Motor Company as it sought to move its culture from "command and control" to a more participative style. In the late 1980's DTA expanded its work to other companies and organizations. The methodology has evolved over the past decade through the work of Dannemiller, Paul Tolchinsky, Roland Loup and other DTA partners. The result is a flexible and comprehensive approach to change management. *Whole-Scale* expands the thinking of *Real Time Strategic Change* and *Real Time Work Design* previously developed by DTA.

Whole-Scale methodology is used in a variety of applications including strategic planning, work design, re-engineering, training and culture change. Robust, repeatable processes allow organizations to:

- Clarify their current reality (including the drivers for change)
- Shape a vision for the organization they are striving to become

- Develop action plans that move them toward that future
- Address information, process, structure and relationship issues vital to the change process

The core *Whole-Scale* competency is around planning and facilitating large whole-system meetings as the key link in the change process. These sessions allow a "critical mass" of the organization (or a sub-system within the organization) to define the criteria for the new team-based culture while experiencing it directly. *Whole-Scale* is a model for what the change can look like and the vehicle by which a paradigm shift is accomplished. Participants experience working in teams to do real work in *Whole-Scale* events.

The term *Whole-Scale* was chosen to reflect the need to address the whole system regardless of the scale (large or small group) at which work was being done. *Whole-Scale* sessions can create "critical moments" in the change process but only in the context of a sound change strategy that includes clear strategic goals, strong leadership alignment, adequate training and concerted implementation follow-through.

Roles of Pre-Event Teams

Planning for the June 13-14 event began in early April. Ferranti-Packard identified a hotel in nearby Niagara Falls that could accommodate 250-300 people and contracted for the space. The most important planning task was the design of what would happen in the event. Two teams played complementary roles in that design, the Leadership Team and the Event Planning Team (also called the Design Team). A third team, the Logistics Team, was responsible for staging the event and seeing to it that it was "seamless" for participants. Finally, the team of three DTA consultants facilitated the design and planning of the event.

Leadership Team

It is critical in any change process that the leadership team be predictable to each other and the organization so that they send consistent messages of support and direction throughout the change process. Without clear sponsorship and participation by leadership, the change effort cannot succeed.

The Leadership Team was comprised of Pierre, his direct reports and the leaders of the three union locals. It was critical for the success of this event that leaders from both the labor and management sides were seen as acting together to support the effort. The team's first responsibility was to prepare the draft strategic plan which would be presented to the entire organization in the event. That work was complete. The next task was to identify a representative microcosm of the plant to serve as the Event Planning Team. We asked for a cross-section of the entire organization including all levels and all functions including some union and management. 23 people were selected including the presidents of the three union locals in the plant.

Finally, the Leadership Team needed to decide how much authority it was willing to give the Design Team and the entire organization in developing the strategic plan. They decided that they were willing to receive input on every part of the draft strategic plan with the understanding that the Leadership Team had to have ultimate control over what went into the final draft of the plan..

Event Planning Team (Design Team)

The Dannemiller Tyson approach to designing and holding large scale interactive meetings relies heavily on working with an Event Planning Team(EPT) or Design Team. This team is active throughout the planning process and during the event itself. At Ferranti-Packard, the team continued to play a role during implementation. Generally, one day of planning with the EPT is required for each day of the actual event. In this case, the Event Planning Team met on May 30-31, two weeks before the large group session.

The Event Planning Team's job is to figure out both *what* needs to be discussed at the large-scale meeting and *how* it should be discussed; but it is difficult (if not impossible) to be responsible for the content and the process at the same time. We complicate the matter further by working with the EPT by consensus. We do not have the "right" design until everybody agrees. Given all that, we have found it particularly important to be clear about roles. As external consultants, we see ourselves as "process" experts; while the Event Planning Team members are the "content" experts. If we can keep our roles clear, a consensus process will result in a most effective design by linking what the process experts know about how to do this kind of session with what the content experts know about the company. By using similar processes and the same underlying principles during the planning as we use during the large-scale event, the Event Planning Team's reactions help determine what will and will not work. Their experience is a constant reality check on the developing design.

The Ferranti-Packard Event Planning Team meeting began with the 23 members sitting at three round tables of seven or eight, just as participants would in the large-scale event. Seating had been assigned to make each table a microcosm of the whole team. The team received a clear charter from Pierre about its role and authority. As individuals, as tables and as an entire team, they built a common database about the company, its environment and what was working and not working. By the end of two days, the people on the team had a new understanding and appreciation of each other. Many on the team had worked at Ferranti-Packard for many years and recalled with pride the days when their plant was a top competitor in their industry. They discovered that, despite their apparent differences, they all wanted the same thing.

They united around that common yearning to be great again, to be part of a company they could be truly proud of. They became a team while working on a purpose statement and agenda outlining the basic flow of the large group event.

The team decided on what needed to happen and in what order things needed to happen. The team decided to invite an industry expert and a panel of current and former customers to give their input to the planning process. They wanted to see Pierre and his entire leadership team present the draft plan for input to show that they were all behind this process. They decided to invite the plant's suppliers to be participants at the tables. And, they decided to invite all of the workers then on indefinite layoff to come, believing that they also had a stake in the outcome and should have a voice in making decisions. The team even undertook to organize the "max-mix" seating chart for the event, deciding how to make each of the 36 tables a the best possible microcosm. By the afternoon of the second day, the team was working on its own and the three consultants simply stepped back and got out of the way.

When the work was done, the team was excited because they knew the design was one of their own choosing. They saw the world in a different way and were anxious to have everyone in the organization have the same experience. At the close of the meeting, each person was asked what they would tell people back in the plant when asked what had happened in these two days. Mark Renner, the shop floor union local president and a vocal skeptic when we began, replied, "They will ask me if we have gotten in bed with management and I will tell them we own half the bed."

Event Logistics Team

To have a successful *Whole-Scale* change meeting, it is particularly important that the activities flow like clockwork: that all the meeting components - participants, speakers, consultants and materials - are where they are needed, when they are needed. The alternative would be seen by participants as chaos. They would either feel "herded around" or they would feel that no one is in charge and therefore, the meeting was not important. A well-organized, well-briefed logistics team is needed to carry out the behind-the-scene activities that take place to ensure the meeting runs smoothly. This includes administrative matters as well.

The eight members of the team were volunteers from outside of the plant. (Being a logistics team member is a full-time job during the event and can't be done by participants.) Some team members came from other locations within Ferranti-Packard or other divisions of Rolls-Royce. Some were outside consultants seeking a chance to experience the *Whole-Scale* method firsthand. They came together to begin work on Staging Day, the day before the large-group event.

DTA Consulting Team

The consulting team consisted of Kathie Dannemiller, Al Blixt and Mary Eggers. Kathie and I were responsible for contact with the leadership team and facilitating the Event Planning Team meeting and the large group meeting itself. At Ferranti-Packard, the role of logistics "tzar" was filled by DTA consultant Mary Eggers. She was in charge of forming and leading the logistics team. She also was responsible for all negotiations about room set-up, meals and other arrangements with the hotel facility. All three consultants worked together to develop the detailed design "script" for the actual event.

Event Purpose and Design

The purpose and agenda below shows the outline of the event as drafted by the Event Planning Team. Each participant had a copy at their place when the event began. A minute-by-minute detailed design was developed by the consultants.

Ferranti-Packard Large Scale Event—Approximately 250 participants including all employees plus previously laid off employees and 22 suppliers.

Purpose:

To work together as a Ferranti-Packard team to become the #1 competitor in our industry by agreeing on:

- o Where we are
- o Where we want to be, and by committing to
- o How we are going to get there as individuals and as a whole

Day 1- Key Activities

7:30 am Welcome

Purpose and Agenda

Table Introductions

Industry Trends

Customer Panel

Organizational Diagnosis

Leadership View

Input on Draft Strategy

4:00 pm Adjourn

Day 2 – Key Activities

7:30 am Revised Strategy Statement

Goals: Preferred Futures

Preferred Futuring

"Systemwide Action Planning

Vote and Lunch

Cross-functional Feedback

Back Home Planning

Evaluation

4:00 pm Adjourn

Roles of Teams During the Event

Table Teams

The flow of activities in a *Whole-Scale* event is from the individual to the table to the whole room. Each max-mix table of eight is the basic unit of work during the event. Each table has its own flip chart pad and markers. By the end of the event, the walls are covered with the work product from the tables. Each table is self-facilitated with roles of facilitator, recorder and reporter being rotated for each new activity. Each person can experience leading the team at some point. Because each table has representatives from all parts of the organization, similar conversations take place at each table. The room is brought whole through methods such as call-outs, report-outs, voting or just getting up and wandering around to look at the work done at other tables.

Leadership Team

It is important to note that all of the leadership team, including Pierre, sat at tables and participated in all activities with the rest of the organization. On the afternoon of Day One, Pierre and the team presented the draft strategic goals and answered questions from the tables. In the next activity, each of the tables provided input on changes, additions or deletions they would like to see in the mission, vision and goals. Then the whole room voted on which suggestions they agreed with most. The Leadership Team took this input and stayed late in the evening of Day One to rewrite the strategy. This act of transformational leadership was one of their key roles in the event. A copy of the revised strategy was at every place the next morning when the team presented its work. Finally, Pierre and the team were responsible for publicly committing to what would be done following the meeting.

Functional Teams

At specific points during the design, people who work together gathered as functional teams to do certain kinds of work, including back home planning. One of the key times when functional groups meet is to process "Valentines" which is our name for cross-functional feedback. At Ferranti-Packard there were 24 functional groups identified. Each max-mix table sent a "valentine" to each functional group telling it what it needed to do differently if they were to achieve their goals. Public commitments from the functional groups about what they would do differently formed a key part of the post-event accountability structure.

Event Planning Team

Members of the Event Planning Team were distributed among the tables as participants. They were the eyes and ears of the consultants during the day to give feed back about the flow of the event. At the end of Day One, Event Planning Team members sat down with the consultants and members of leadership to read participant evaluations and advise on any needed changes in the design for the next day. At the end of Day Two, EPT members provided their insights into the event and what was needed to implement the plan. The group had worked so well together that they reformed at the end of nine months to research the status of plan commitments from the functional groups. (see appendix).

Logistics Team

The Logistics Team managed every aspect of the physical environment to make sure everything worked for participants. On the staging day, team members went through the detailed design with the consultants and decided on what roles each would play. Operating from a "war room" next door, the Logistics Team managed seating of participants, greeting and guiding outside speakers, handling wireless microphones and distributed handouts and assignments to the tables on a just-in-time basis. The team managed the production and distribution of the revised strategic plan between Day One and Day Two. They even would "sweep" the halls to get participants back from breaks and lunch on time. Their work day began at 6:00 AM and ended at midnight.

Consulting Team

The role of the consulting team facilitating the event is to provide the minimum structure necessary to allow the participants to have the right conversation at each point in the event. One consultant is usually "up front" facilitating a given activity while the other monitors the energy in the room to make sure the event is working. When an activity runs long (because the right work is being done) the consultants must redesign the remaining activities to fit the time available. When something isn't working for participants, the consultants must know when to step in and change the activity. Continuous conversation between the consultants and the logistics tzar are necessary to monitor and adjust the flow of the day.

Event Outcomes

The first and perhaps most important outcome of this meeting was that the people of Ferranti-Packard saw the world in a different way when it was over. They had heard an industry expert tell them that their market was not growing and their competitors were producing better quality faster and at lower cost. They heard from their customers. One ex-customer (which had taken Ferranti-Packard off their bid list because of poor quality) told the 280 people in the room, "We're not trying to put you folks out of business. You are doing that job yourselves." But, then another major customer, Westinghouse, told them, "I am building power plants around the world that will pay a premium for fast installation. If you can shorten your delivery times from 28 weeks nearer the industry standard of 20 weeks, I can fill your plant." If there was a single turning point in the event, it was at that moment.

You could almost feel the atmosphere change as each person wondered how to get eight weeks out of the order-to-delivery cycle. They realized almost immediately that there were many places they could speed things up if they improved the way in which the various departments worked together to process orders. Orders from the sales department might sit for days or weeks in engineering before drawing were ready for the shop floor. Similar delays were found in the hand-offs between engineering and purchasing, purchasing and manufacturing, etc.. In short, nearly everyone in the room suddenly discovered there was something they could do; but only if they could improve interdepartmental cooperation

The tangible "deliverable" of the event was a working strategy for the plant that everyone understood and had a hand in creating. There were nearly 100 specific public commitments for action from the 24 functional groups, including the suppliers group and the Leadership Team. People began acting out of the new strategy even before they left the meeting. This was demonstrated by conversations that were happening around the room and in the halls during breaks. Workers from different departments were talking about how to work better together. Suppliers were in conversations with workers from the shop floor about how to serve their needs better.

The intangible outcome was just as important. As the Event Planning Team had wanted, the participants had worked "together as a Ferranti-Packard team" taking responsibility for shaping and moving toward their shared vision of the future.

Role of Post-Event Teams

The place where most strategic plans fail is in implementation. For this plan to succeed, several key teams needed to follow through on the new strategy the group had created.

Functional Teams

Because the strategic planning had been tied directly to functional work groups, each area of the plant had specific action plans to work on. Many of these plans involved improving communication and cooperation with other areas of the organization.

Ad Hoc Task Teams

Some work coming out of the event was assigned to one of several task teams that were formed to tackle issues that involved more than one department.

Leadership Team

In addition to their own commitments, the Leadership Team was responsible for maintaining and supporting the implementation effort. That included communications that would keep everyone informed on progress as well as responding to the greatly increased demand for training programs. Finally, the Leadership Team was responsible for making the case to Rolls-Royce for some much-needed investment in new plant equipment based on the new strategy. Representatives from Rolls-Royce had been present at the event and were favorably impressed with the direction that the plant had taken.

Event Planning Team

The Event Planning Team was reluctant to disband. While their official work was complete, they had formed strong ties with each other. As a group, they took it upon themselves nine months later to monitor progress on the plan.

Results After One Year

By June, 1997, the future of Ferranti-Packard at St. Catharines looked very different:

- Cycle times for product delivery had been reduced from 27-28 weeks to 18-19 weeks making the plant "world class" in that category.

- The cost of quality (scrap, rework) had been reduced from 8.6% in 1995 of sales to 3.4% in 1996. The new goal is to reduce that figure to 1.5% of sales.

- Sales were up from $40M in 1995 to a projected $50M in 1996 and $60M in 1997.

- A new program to involve shop floor employees to lead plant tours received rave reviews from prospective customers and actually resulted into orders in several cases.

- Cross-functional problem-solving teams were formed to involve shop floor employees in addressing long standing process problems in the plant.

- In the Spring of 1997, all three locals of the United Steel Workers agreed to new three year contracts that included more flexibility in job classifications (which management wanted) and an early retirement option for senior workers (which the union wanted).

- Union grievances have dropped significantly in the plant.

- After losing $5.5 million in 1995, the plant trimmed that to $1.5 million in 1996 and expects to break even or be in the black for 1997.

- All laid off workers have been called back and the

plant has increased its total workforce by 20% in the past year, accepting applications for new employees for the first time in this decade.

• 25% of all workers in the plant are currently training for new jobs or responsibilities.

• And finally, Rolls-Royce has approved investment in major new plant equipment based on the improvement in financial performance.

For the people of Ferranti-Packard, the "event" of June 1996 was a turning point in their history. It was not because some outside expert told them what to do. It was not because they had leaders who knew all the answers. It was a turning point because they discovered the power of working together with shared information and shared goals as a single empowered team.

Chapter Two

What Leaders Get Wrong About Vision: Seven Vision Mistakes and How To Avoid Them

By Albert B. Blixt

Many years ago, I was about to take a position leading an organization for the first time. I went to an executive I respected and asked him what I needed to know to be a good leader. His response was, "You've got to have a vision. The Leader has to have a vision."

I have since learned that advice was only partly correct. It is not enough that the leader has a vision. You need the right kind of vision and it has to be shared.

In his book Fatal Illusions, author James Lucas wrote, "Vision is the quality that elevates the mundane into higher realms of achievement. Vision excites passion, brings meaning to otherwise routine or dreary tasks, gives direction to goals, and provides guidance for daily decisions. Without vision, organizations wither, and people lose interest. Yet most organizations don't have it."

After two decades coaching leaders and helping organizations create strategic plans, let me share seven key mistakes that leaders too often make.

Mistake #1: Confusing Mission and Vision

A mission statement tells *who we are* and what business we are in. It defines who we serve and what value we create for those stakeholders. Mission tells what we stand for, the values that we will uphold even when the going gets tough.

Vision, on the other hand, tells *where we want to go*. It is what we aspire to become in the future; the possibility that we are reaching for, stretching for, that motivates what we do. When we confuse mission and vision, we confuse ourselves, and our co-workers, as well as those we serve.

The most important aspect of an inspiring vision is storytelling. Vision tells a story about the future that we aspire to create in a way that is relatable to everyone in the organization. A great vision inspires great stories, stories that move the heart.

Stories can engage, inspire, and change even the most sophisticated and skeptical personalities. The simpler the story, the wider the appeal and often the deeper the impact. Many people simply won't invest at a visceral emotional level unless the message is in story form. Vision statements, to be worth anything, have to differentiate our organization from the competition so that anyone who interfaces with our organization will be able to identify the statement with us even if our name or logo isn't at the top of the page.

> *Question for leaders: Take a look at your vision statement. Is it inspiring and energizing. Does it tell a story you want to be part of?*

Mistake #2: Thinking Vision Is a Bumper Sticker

Very often in the strategic plan, organizations will have a short, pithy 5-to-7 word vision statement that they believe will make a good slogan — a good way of remembering what the organization aspires to be. In fact, such a short statement has almost nothing to do with reality.

The difference between a vision that inspires and a vision that goes up on the wall or on a coffee mug, is the ability of that statement to paint a picture of possibility that will cause people to say, "I want to be a part of creating that!"

Ron Lippitt, one of the early pioneers of systems change theory, wrote an article called *"Future Before You Plan."* In it he coined the term "preferred future." Preferred futuring asks clients to imagine they could travel ahead in time 3–5 years and see what it would look like if their goals had been achieved. The vision puts us vividly in that preferred future picture.

If you can put your vision statement on a bumper sticker it's too short. Vision is a picture of the future that draws us, pulls us, into the future with enough detail to make it real.

We don't know who we are because we've developed a vision statement; we know because we live who we are. That means taking the time to work through the clichés to get to the core of what's important to all of our stakeholders. Brief vision statements are invariably non-directive. A one sentence vision statement gives the illusion of saying something when it has all the substance of a cloud. It needs to have enough detail to give guidance to the planning process. It has to flow from our understanding of the daily life of our employees, customers, distributors, and suppliers. All of our most important values ought to be reflected and given life in our vision statement.

> *Lesson for Leaders: Look at your vision statement again, and this time see if you can visualize the future. What does "better" look like?*

Mistake #3: Thinking You Don't Need a Vision at All

Some leaders have the idea that you don't need a vision. "Just do your job" is their motto and the rest will take care of itself. Without a vision, effort is scattered, and people will set their priorities based on what they think is best for themselves and their team.

Empowering people, ordinarily a good thing, when there's no unifying vision only leads empire building, silo creation and the diffusion of energy. It also leads to a "ready, fire, aim" reactive approach and a flavor of the month fixation with whatever seems to be in fashion at the moment. We need to keep in mind that making a profit is a result of good leadership, not a vision or a goal. Lack of vision also leads to a kind of disabling inertia caused by people moving in different directions. To fight this that we must think differently.

This lack of direction and aspiration is most often found in organizations that have been successful in the past and are playing not to lose instead of playing to win. This has been true in American higher education now struggling with disruptive change as well as large previously successful companies.

The U.S. auto industry in the 1990's was losing market share to foreign car makers and while they were worried, there was no vision of what success would look like after decades of dominating the domestic market. When I was consulting to the auto industry at that time, there was an obsession with "taking cost out" as a strategy. Not very inspiring.

Eventually both GM and Chrysler were forced into bankruptcy and Ford barely avoided it. That near death experience, new leadership, and a change of mindset has renewed the vision of the car business. Now these companies tell a story of being in the mobility business instead of the car business. They have embraced the move to autonomous, electric vehicles and the result is a new burst of innovation.

Lesson for Leaders: Have you treated your vision statement as an afterthought or as the unifying story that engages hearts and minds?

Mistake #4: Thinking Bigger is Better

Leaders who think that growth is an end in itself are making a mistake. Think BlockBuster Video, Borders Books, and a host of others who have fueled growth that was not sustainable. Many executives at fortune 1000 companies have said that growth was their most important goal. After all, growth keeps the stock price going up. However, growth is a miserable measure of success.

Bigger is not necessarily better. Better is better.

That means creating value for all stakeholders. The obsession with growth leads to an acquisition strategy to capture top line revenue, often at the expense of organic growth, innovation, and sustainability. Growth is a result, not a goal. There are lots of ways to be #1. Being number one in quality, number one in consumer value, number one in employee retention, or number one in industry innovation are better goals than being number one in sales.

Unfortunately, executives are often compensated based on their ability to generate quarter-over- quarter growth in revenue and so they pursue strategies that create short-term gains at the expense of longer-term sustainability. Of course, we want our organizations to grow; but by what measure?

An organization may need to grow to achieve some economies of scale that make it competitive in the marketplace. An organization may need to grow to reach new markets. Obsession with growth for its own sake, regardless of the means or method is not likely to end well. Growth has multiple meanings. It can mean getting bigger, but it also can mean developing more complex connections and more agility. The growth of an organization can be the mark of its maturity as well as of its size.

Lesson for leaders: What is your definition of the role of growth in your strategy?

Mistake #5: Thinking Vision Must Have Lofty Platitudes

One of the most common mistakes about vision is the belief that the statement must speak in abstract global concepts.

IKEA, for instance, says its vision is, "to create a better everyday life for many people." Hilton Hotels says its vision is, "to fill the earth with the light and warmth of hospitality." Both of these are nice sentiments; but do they speak to the people that do the work every day? How do these visions describe a world that is different from the present?

Compare those with the vision statement of Southwest Airlines, "to become the world's most loved, most flown, and most profitable airline." When I worked for Chrysler years ago, the vision statement was, "to be the company that makes the cars people choose to buy, love to drive, and want to buy again."

Notice that these last two are grounded in the work of the organization. Lofty language often has no meaning for customers or employees. While we may think that we've produced a masterpiece for the ages, what that language evokes on the frontline is indifference or ridicule.

Lesson for leaders: Is your vision of the future anchored to your mission? Will your people believe it? Will they commit to achieving it?

Mistake #6: Thinking that Everyone Understands the Vision

A survey asked executives what their greatest challenges were. The number one answer: "Getting the vision to the front line."

As leaders, we see the big picture. We have access to lots of information, so the future of the organization seems obvious to us. Down in the weeds, things are different.

The priorities and interests of the people who work for

and around us are as varied as their personalities, needs, and desires. We must look past their seeming agreement to the reality of what they really need and want. We can't connect our organizational priorities with what people see as important until we know what their priorities really are.

If we create conditions where an individual must choose between their personal career goals and supporting the organizational vision, they will choose the former every time. Our work as leaders must align individual interests of our people with the collective vision for our organization. Yes, communication is essential; but what we really need is two-way communication. For leaders, the ability to listen can be the most powerful tool in the toolkit.

Getting people to support the vision is a process that has distinct stages that each person must pass through. These are five stages on the adoption path:

- Awareness — I've heard about it
- Understanding — I know what it is all about
- Belief — I think it is a good idea
- Compliance — I will do what is asked of me
- Commitment — I will do what it takes to make it happen!

Lesson for leaders: How much do you know about where different people are on the path to commitment? How can you help them move toward commitment?

Mistake #7: Thinking That We As Leaders Must Create The Vision

If we want vision to mean something, we shouldn't "issue" a vision statement. We should ask for people's input to get both their input and their "buy-in." Then we have to do the hard work of working it through together. Vision does not come by inspiration; it comes from knowledge intelligently cultivated.

If a vision doesn't inspire our people to do something greater than we are already doing, it isn't really a vision at all, and we should admit it.

To lead an effective vision development process, don't assume to know what employees and customers want from leadership. We should assume that we don't know, and we probably don't. So, we have to ask.

Wise leaders involve everybody because we know how easily our biases and preconceived ideas can cause us to mislead ourselves.

Employees, consumers, and vendors are not usually involved in this process, nor is their input welcome. What we ask for is "buy-in". The best we can hope for is compliance and not commitment. Vision is how we connect individual purpose and meaning to the organizational future we're trying to create together.

One of the most neglected components of vision is feedback. How do people feel about it? Do they care? Do they think it relates to customers? Is their visceral reaction to say "wow," or to make cynical comments? Feedback is an indispensable part of the communications loop. Leaders have an obligation to make certain that not only is the vision worth embracing, but that our people are eager to keep it alive every day.

Lesson for Leaders: Do you believe that people support what they help to create? What are you doing to practice that belief?

Final Thoughts: The Leader's Vision Checklist

Here are five questions to ask about your vision statement:

1. Is it big enough? Does it speak to the possibility of doing something to make the world a better place?

2. Is it inspiring? Does it energize people and make them want to work to achieve it?

3. Is it a stretch, but possible? Does it pull us into the future with a promise of something great? I often ask clients, "Where is the call to greatness?"

4. Is it grounded in the mission? Does it speak in enough detail so that people can see themselves in it?

5. Does it invite sharing? Will people be proud enough to enroll others in working on the vision?

If you are able to answer yes to all of these questions, you will have taken the first step to becoming a truly visionary leader.

The next step is to develop a plan to move your organization toward that vision. But that is a conversation for another day.

Chapter Three

Overcoming the Imposter Within: Proven Tactics for Achieving Excellence for New Leaders

By Jeffrey Edwards

When the Room Doesn't Feel Like Yours

It doesn't always happen with a formal announcement or a grand promotion. Sometimes, leadership sneaks up on you. One day, you're quietly doing your job, following the routine. The next, you're being asked to lead a project, guide a team, or make a critical decision. And just like that, the predictable rhythm of your work life shifts. The quiet comfort of routine gives way to the weight of responsibility.

You might find yourself thinking, "Wait—how did I get here?" "Am I really the right person for this?" If that sounds familiar, you're not alone. Many leaders—especially those who didn't plan to lead—experience this moment of disorientation. It's often accompanied by a persistent, nagging voice that questions your worth, your readiness, your right to be in the room.

That voice has a name: Imposter Syndrome.

The backstory of "Imposter Syndrome"

The concept of "Imposter Syndrome" emerged from a

groundbreaking 1978 study by psychologists Pauline Rose Clance and Suzanne Imes. (Clance, 1978). Originally presented as "imposter phenomenon", it revealed the disconnect between external success and internal self-perception. In their research study of 150 high-achieving women in academia, they discovered these accomplished professionals often attributed their success to luck or circumstance rather than acknowledging their own skills and hard work.

Recent studies highlight the prevalence of this challenge. A 2025 global study by Strengthscope found that the perception gap between how leaders rate their effectiveness compared to their teams' perceptions has grown by 75% since 2019. This widening gap suggests that leaders, especially new ones, are increasingly underestimating their own abilities and impact.

Journey of Discovery

Picture this: a young, university-educated Black man working in a global IT company. That was me, suddenly thrust into a leadership role. No formal training. No roadmap. Just a new title and a seat at the table.

The meeting rooms felt unfamiliar, almost alien. I noticed the subtle glances, the raised eyebrows from seasoned executives who seemed to question my presence. I could feel the unspoken doubts hanging in the air—Does he belong here? Is he ready?

Every meeting felt like a test. Every presentation, a performance. I second-guessed my decisions, over-prepared for every conversation, and hesitated to speak unless I was absolutely sure. I worked long hours, not just to meet expectations, but to prove—mostly to myself—that I deserved to be there.

Have you ever felt that way? Like you're a respected, capable professional on the outside, but inside, you're bracing for someone to discover you're not as competent as they think?

That's imposter syndrome. And for me, it was amplified by being one of the few people of color in leadership. I wasn't just navigating the usual pressures of the role—I was carrying the weight of representation, of proving that I belonged in spaces where people like me were rarely seen.

It's worth noting that these feelings of self-doubt are non-exclusive to any group. Take Albert Einstein, for instance. Despite his groundbreaking contributions to physics, he once confided, "The exaggerated esteem in which my lifework is held makes me very ill at ease. I feel compelled to think of myself as an involuntary swindler." This sentiment from one of the greatest minds in science underscores how pervasive and powerful imposter syndrome can be, affecting leaders across various fields and levels of achievement.

The Turning Point – The Value of a Mentor

My breakthrough didn't come from a leadership seminar or a performance review. It came from a person—my mentor, Talisha (not her real name).

Talisha had walked a path like mine. She was also a person of color navigating the tech industry, and she understood the unspoken pressures I was facing. She didn't just offer advice—she offered perspective. She saw through the mask I was wearing and gently called out what I couldn't yet name: "You're not an imposter. You're just growing into your power."

And there were other times when her feedback or words felt harsh but rang true: "If you want a career here, that's on you." Through our conversations, Talisha exposed my personal dismissals (aka "B.S.") and reframed my doubts. While real, they were only part of the story. She expanded the landscape through which I saw my world of work. She emphasized the importance of taking action and being open to feedback, showing me how these practices could transform self-doubt into growth opportunities.

"Your background, your voice, and your lived experience aren't liabilities," she would constantly remind me when she heard the fear in my voice.

Talisha's wisdom extended beyond personal reassurance. She challenged me to think bigger: "If you want to thrive in this company, you need to expand your view of your impact and influence. Think on a scale larger than you've ever imagined before."

This shift changed everything. I stopped trying to prove I belonged and started focusing on my unique contributions. I engaged more consistently with senior executives, team members, and peers. Over time, new opportunities emerged – from local to national to global. Every new role or task became a new challenge and opportunity to learn. Success became a team accomplishment instead of a solo project. After 2.5 years, it was starting to make sense!

Then one day, Talisha left the company. I initially felt adrift. But her impact endured. Her mentorship had equipped me to lead larger projects and navigate senior-level interactions with confidence. Twenty-five years later, her words still resonate.

From Self-Doubt to Self-Mastery: Practical Strategies

So how do you move from questioning your worth to leading with confidence? The journey isn't about eliminating self-doubt entirely—it's about learning to lead through it. Here are the strategies that helped me, and that I now share with others on their leadership path:

1. Acknowledge the Voice of Doubt

   Imposter syndrome thrives in silence. The first step is to recognize it when it shows up. Give it a name. Say it out loud. Write it down. But don't let it define you.

2. Reframe the Narrative

   Instead of seeing challenges as proof that you're unqualified, view them as signs that you're growing.

3. Celebrate Small Wins

   Progress is movement toward your goals. Keep a journal of your wins—big or small: That email you finally sent; that important meeting you led; the moment you made spoke up - they all count. Over time, these small victories become the foundation of confidence.

4. Find Mentors and Allies

   You don't have to do this alone. Seek out mentors who understand your journey. Build a support network of peers who can offer perspective, encouragement, and accountability.Your network is your safety net—and your launchpad.

5. Embrace Your Unique Perspective

   Your background, your story, your lens on the world—they're not obstacles. They're your edge. The more you lean into what makes you different, the more powerful your leadership becomes.

6. Practice Self-Compassion

   You're not expected to be perfect. Leadership is messy, human, and evolving. Treat yourself with the same kindness and patience you'd offer a friend navigating self-doubt.

7. Adopt a Growth Mindset

   As psychologist Carol Dweck's research shows, believing that you can grow and improve is a game-changer. Mistakes become lessons. Feedback becomes fuel. And challenges become steppingstones.

From Inner Confidence to Team Excellence

As you begin to lead with greater self-awareness, something powerful happens: your growth starts to ripple outward. The more grounded and authentic you become, the more your team feels it—and responds to it.

Here's how your personal transformation translates into building a high-performance, highly engaged team:

Authentic Leadership Builds Trust

When you're honest about your own challenges and growth, you create a culture of openness. Your team sees that it's okay to not have all the answers. That vulnerability builds trust—and trust is the foundation of high performance.

Engagement Through Delegation

As your confidence grows, so does your ability to delegate. Stop trying to do everything yourself and start empowering others to step up. This not only lightens your load—it helps your team members grow, take ownership, engage and feel valued.

Leveraging Diverse Strengths

Self-aware leaders are better at recognizing the unique strengths of each team member. Begin to see your team not as a group of roles, but as a collection of talents, perspectives, and potential. That's when collaboration becomes powerful.

Constructive, Compassionate Feedback

When you've done the inner work, you're better equipped to give feedback that's both honest and supportive. Understand that feedback isn't about judgment—it's about growth. And your team will feel that difference.

Fostering Innovation Through Psychological Safety

Teams thrive when they feel safe to take risks, share ideas, and even fail. Your willingness to be real and human creates an environment where innovation can flourish—because people aren't afraid to try.

Celebrating Collective Wins

When you're no longer consumed by self-doubt, you can genuinely celebrate your team's success. Recognition becomes more than a task—it becomes a habit. And that boosts morale, motivation, and momentum.

Leading Forward: From Self-Awareness to Lasting Impact

Your journey from self-doubt to high performance isn't just about personal growth—it's about creating a ripple effect. When you lead with authenticity, courage, and self-awareness, you give others permission to do the same.

Leadership isn't about having all the answers. It's about creating the conditions where the best answers can emerge—often from the most unexpected places. By confronting imposter syndrome and embracing your unique perspective, you're not just becoming a better leader. You're shaping a more inclusive, resilient, and high-performing culture.

Your Next Steps

As a new manager or emerging leader, remember: Your leadership journey is just beginning, and it will be filled with challenges and triumphs.

By applying these strategies and embracing your unique voice, you're paving the way for a new generation of authentic, confident leaders who will drive real change and impact in their organizations and communities.

Embrace the journey, learn from every experience, and remember: the best is yet to come.

Chapter Four

New Horizons: Navigating the Growing Pains of Leadership for Emerging Leaders

By Jeffrey Edwards

The familiar chime of a virtual meeting echoed through my office. As the screen illuminated, Tyrone's (not his real name) face appeared - a talented, self-driven professional. It's amazing to believe that just twelve months prior, our paths crossed through a mentoring program by the Black Professionals Technical Network's (BPTN) Mentoring initiative that would shape our professional journeys.

As his video came online, his facial expression reflected both confidence and uncertainty today, which piqued my curiosity for what was to come.

"Coach, I'm glad we could connect,"Tyrone began, his voice carrying a hint of nervous energy. "These past few weeks have been... intense."

I smiled encouragingly. "Ahh, sounds like there's a story here. Why don't you walk me through what's been happening?"

Tyrone took a deep breath, his shoulders visibly relaxed as he prepared to share his thoughts. "Well, now that I have been promoted to a manager role, I'm finding myself in situations I've never faced before. It's like I've stepped into a whole new world," he said, his voice tinged with excitement and apprehension.

"Go on," I said with a grin. "Leadership often comes with growing pains. Let's unpack some of these challenges."

Tyrone nodded, his brow slightly furrowing as he considered his next words. "Right now, I must prepare a performance plan for my team for senior management. I used to be a peer with these people, and now I'm supposed to assess their work. It feels... uncomfortable," he admitted, his voice carrying a hint of uncertainty. His mind raced as he thought about the potential impact of his evaluations on his relationships with his team. Would they see him as a fair leader or someone who had changed?

I leaned forward in my chair, my interest piqued. "That is a significant shift," I said, my tone encouraging, "How are you approaching it?"

"That's just it," Tyrone said, frustration creeping into his voice. "I'm not sure how! I want to maintain the positive relationships I've built, but I also need to provide honest assessments to upper management. It feels like I'm caught between two worlds."

"It's a challenge for sure. Transitioning into leadership, especially when your peers are now your direct reports can be ...as you said, 'uncomfortable,'" I replied. "What would be helpful for you today?"

Tyrone's eyes peered up to the top of his office, appearing he was searching for the answer on the ceiling. As his gaze returned to the camera, I said: "how about we break it down a bit?" Tyrone's eyes lit up, grateful for the direction. "Yes," he said enthusiastically.

"Okay, let's start...what specific concerns do you have about the performance evaluation process?" I asked.

"Well, I'm worried that being too critical might damage the relationships I've built. But I'm not doing my job properly if I'm too lenient."

"Got it," I replied, leaning closer to the camera. "Here's another perspective to consider: Your leadership role isn't separate from those relationships you've built. It's an extension of them." As I spoke, I hoped my words would resonate with Tyrone and help him see the value in his new role.

Tyrone's eyebrows raised slightly, a sign that he was intrigued.

"Think about it this way," I continued, "if you truly care about your team members' growth and success, wouldn't you want to provide them with honest, constructive feedback?"

As I posed the question, I saw Tyrone's mind working through the implications. He seemed to be grappling with the idea of balancing honesty with empathy.

The Performance Evaluation Predicament

Tyrone's first challenge was clear: he was grappling with the daunting task of conducting performance evaluations for his new team. The weight of this responsibility seemed to hang heavily on his shoulders.

"I feel like I'm ambushing them," Tyrone confessed, his brow furrowed. "How can I evaluate their entire year's performance in one sitting?"

I nodded, understanding his concern. "Tyrone, here's a crucial leadership lesson," I said, leaning forward. "No one should be surprised in an annual performance evaluation. These conversations should be a summary of ongoing dialogues you've had throughout the year."

His eyes widened with realization. "But how do I make that happen?"

"It starts with your one-on-ones," I explained, shifting the focus to practical steps. "These regular check-ins are not just about task updates; they're opportunities for continuous feedback and growth discussions."

The No-Surprise Principle

Tyrone nodded slowly, absorbing the information. "That makes sense. But how do I ensure there are no surprises during the evaluation?"

I smiled, appreciating his quick grasp of the concept. "That's the key, Tyrone. No one should ever be surprised during a performance evaluation. If they are, it means you haven't been doing your job as a leader throughout the year."

Tyrone's expression shifted to one of concern. "That's a lot of pressure," he admitted, feeling the weight of his new responsibilities.

As he spoke, Tyrone couldn't help but think about the expectations placed on him. The fear of letting his team down gnawed at him, making him question whether he was ready for this role.

"It is," I agreed, "but it's also an opportunity. Regular feedback creates trust and opens channels for improvement. It's not about catching people off guard but guiding them towards success." As I spoke, I hoped my words would resonate with Tyrone and help him see the value in his new role.

I remembered my own journey into leadership and the challenges I faced. It was a reminder that growth often comes from discomfort.

"Excellent question," I said, my tone encouraging. "Performance conversations aren't intended to be events that happen once a year."

Tyrone leaned forward; his interest piqued. "What do you mean by that?"

"Think about your one-on-one meetings, Tyrone. How often do you have them? What do you discuss?" I asked, hoping to guide him toward a more effective approach.

As I posed the question, I reflected on the importance of regular check-ins and continuous feedback. It was a lesson I had learned the hard way, and I wanted to ensure Tyrone didn't make the same mistakes.

"Think about your one-on-one meetings, Tyrone. How often do you have them? What do you discuss?"

"We have them bi-weekly," Tyrone replied. "We usually go over current projects, any roadblocks, that sort of thing."

As he spoke, Tyrone realized that his one-on-one meetings could be more than just task updates. He saw the potential for these sessions to become opportunities for growth and development."

"That's a great start," I affirmed. "Now, imagine if these sessions were opportunities for your team members to ask questions, clarify issues or share feedback. How might that change the dynamic of your annual performance evaluations?" As I spoke, I hoped Tyrone would see the value in creating a culture of open communication. It was a crucial aspect of effective leadership, and I wanted him to embrace it.

Tyrone's eyes widened with realization. "They wouldn't come as a surprise," he said slowly. "The team members would already know where they stand." As he spoke, Tyrone felt a sense of relief. He understood that regular feedback could alleviate the pressure of annual evaluations and foster a more supportive environment."

"Exactly!" I exclaimed, feeling a surge of satisfaction at Tyrone's insight. "No one should be surprised in an annual performance evaluation if there have been regular conversations and feedback throughout the year. Creating a workplace culture of open communication and high performance is iterative."

Tyrone listened intently, his posture straightening as he absorbed the advice. "I suppose so," Tyrone nodded slowly. "But how do I do that without coming across as critical or damaging our working relationship?" His earlier nervousness was giving way to thoughtful consideration. "I can see how that would make the process less daunting. But Coach, what if I'm not comfortable giving negative feedback?"

"Tyrone, unfortunately, the term feedback is often associated with something negative. But think of a time when someone told you: 'Great job' or 'Loved your presentation.' Well, guess what? That's also feedback!"

"So, consider this: what if we substituted the term feedback with data?" I asked.

"Good point," he said.

"How does your team's performance grow or improve without feedback? If you don't do your job in providing that guidance, their performance ultimately falls on you," I responded.

Tyrone sat back, absorbing this perspective. I could almost see the gears turning in his mind. "So, by avoiding those potentially uncomfortable conversations, I'm actually doing a disservice to my team?"

"Precisely," I confirmed. "Leadership is more about influence; it's about helping your team grow and succeed. Sometimes, that means having difficult conversations. But when done with genuine care and a focus on improvement, these conversations can strengthen your relationships and boost team performance."

"I think I understand," Tyrone said, his voice gaining confidence. "It's not about being critical but about fostering growth and learning."

Tyrone reflected on this idea. He realized his hesitation to provide feedback stemmed from a desire to maintain harmony. Yet, he understood now that true leadership required honesty and the courage to address issues head-on.

"Exactly," I affirmed. "Now, let's discuss another crucial aspect of your new role."

Dynamics of Managing Up

Tyrone's expression shifted to one of slight discomfort. "Well, before, I'd just report problems up the chain. Now, I'm expected to come up with solutions, too. It's a whole different mindset."

I smiled, recognizing this common hurdle for new leaders. "This shift is a fundamental part of moving into leadership, Tyrone. You're no longer just identifying issues; you're now responsible for offering ideas which require a more strategic approach to thinking."

"How do I develop that kind of thinking?" Tyrone asked eagerly.

"Start by asking yourself a few key questions when faced with a problem," I paused as he grabbed his notebook, ready to take notes.

I continued. "Consider the following questions before you meet with your manager:

- How does this issue impact our goals?
- What resources do we have to address it?
- What are potential solutions, and what are their pros and cons?

By systematically working through these questions, you'll naturally start to think more strategically."

Tyrone's eyes widened with understanding. "I see. It's about stepping back and seeing the bigger picture, right?"

"Precisely," I nodded. "And remember, your recommendations don't always have to be perfect solutions. Sometimes, presenting a well-thought-out plan with options can be just as valuable. It shows you're proactively addressing issues and thinking critically about the business."

As our conversation continued, we delved into other aspects of Tyrone's new role – time management, delegation, and fostering team development. With each topic, I could see Tyrone's confidence growing, his initial apprehension giving way to enthusiasm for the challenges ahead.

Tyrone reflected on everything he had learned. He realized leadership was not just about giving orders, but inspiring and guiding his team toward their full potential.

"Coach, this conversation has been eye-opening," Tyrone said, his voice filled with newfound purpose. "I realize now that becoming a leader isn't just about a new title. It's about developing a new mindset and set of skills."

Accountability Metrics

As our session neared its end, Tyrone's energy had shifted from nervous to determined. "Coach, I've got a lot to work on. How do I make sure I'm staying on track?"

"Have you heard the concept of an accountability metric?" I asked. "After each meeting with your team members, document the following:

- Progress on assigned tasks
- Key discussion points
- Action items for follow-up
- Any performance insights or feedback shared."

Tyrone's eyes lit up. "This is what I need! He realized that by doing so, he would keep his team accountable and himself.

"Exactly," I nodded. "Consistency builds trust. When your team sees you consistently following up and acting on your commitments, it strengthens their faith in your leadership."

"Well, Coach, you've given me a lot of homework!" we both had a good laugh.

I smiled, feeling a sense of pride in Tyrone's growth. "That's exactly right, Tyrone. Consider the current challenges you're facing and your opportunities for growth. Embrace them, learn from them. Leadership is a journey of continuous learning."

I added,"Tyrone, In the end, leadership isn't about perfection but progress. It's about creating an environment where you, as the leader and your team can learn, grow, and achieve their full potential. And that, perhaps, is the most valuable lesson any new leader can learn: today you've taken a significant step in that journey."

"Thanks, Coach. Talk to you in a couple of weeks. Looking forward to sharing my updates," Tyrone replied, as our call ended.

Every Leader Has A Story

Concluding our video call, I found myself contemplating the conversation. Tyrone's narrative resonated deeply, echoing the challenges and growth I've witnessed among emerging leaders throughout my career.

The path from being an individual contributor to assuming a leadership role is seldom straightforward. However, with the right guidance, constructive feedback, and a growth-oriented mindset, this transition can become a profoundly transformative and fulfilling experience.

Chapter Five

On Paying People Fairly

By Dr. Mike Hackney

This story was related to me by one of the executives involved during a consulting assignment. I've left it in the first person, as he told it to me.

How We Got it Wrong

"Gee, Boss—this is all? Thanks for the raise and bonus, I guess!" one of my better managers said in a disappointed voice as we conducted his annual performance review.

I wasn't particularly happy, either. My company was doing everything it could to not retain our good employees.

For all of my direct reports—and for their direct reports, the response was the same: disappointment and disbelief after what had been a really good year for the company. Expectations of individual reward were high, following a year of hard work, extra sacrifice, and tremendous, company leading results for our division. The company had exceeded net-profitability by 12%; our division had exceeded its commitments by 15%. Yet when it came to share the wealth, there was little there as dictated by corporate policy. An average performer received a raise of 1.3%, and above average performer received a raise of 1.5%.

To say my team members were both frustrated at their own compensation and what they could do for their direct reports was an understatement, and it completely undermined the corporate mantra of how *We Truly Care for Our Employees!* Each period and quarter the division members gathered in various groups. Actual performance, compared to targets, were shared and discussed. Opportunities to improve were identified. Those opportunities were then implemented as possible. And over the course of subsequent periods and quarters, the team improved.

The success of the improvement was in the deliverables and performance reports. By the end of the Fiscal year, every target had been met, exceeded by a little, or a couple by a lot. Every financial goal had been exceeded to some degree. The team—from hourlies to management—to executives, felt very positive for their teams, the company, and candidly, their own probable end-of-year compensation.

But when that was shared at the end of the new first quarter, we failed: completely, totally, and unequivocally. Except for one department. Our corporate H.R. team had a made a commitment for their own metrics to not have individual compensation, before bonuses, increase on average any higher than 2.5%. Executive compensation was excluded, of course. None of the C-suite executives responsible for the actual Profit and Loss of the corporation realized that was going on. And in end the vice president of human resources met their goal!

The CEO heard about the disappointment from his other C-suite executives because they'd heard about it from everyone else. We had a great year! What happened to *we care about our employees*? They had no answers and we lower-level folks were told to tell everyone it was being looked into.

Naturally, more than one or two key players at the differing levels of the company—team members, supervisors, managers, and even executives—who, to a person had really gone the extra mile, began (correctly) to question the ethics of the company. They began to question why they would work for a company which didn't live up to its claimed values. And several decided to find new jobs over the next six months. They knew there was a problem and they either didn't desire to see if it was figured out, or didn't want to hang around long enough to find out.

An Honest Question

The CEO of the company was an honest man.

He'd been around a long time and while he was well positioned to retire, he had no desire to do so. A few visits to the field in the month after the annual raises and non-executive bonuses were announced drove it home: he had a problem. His employees had not lost all faith in him, but they'd lost most of it. And he did not like that.

He called the division leaders and C-Suite executives to a meeting and asked one simple question: please explain to me how we had a banner year, the individual divisions did very well, with several far-exceeding the company's goals, and yet our rank-and-file workforce feels betrayed?

There was a lot of hmmmmming and hawwwwwwwing and empty statements by a few of the folks. He didn't accept it. Then he asked again, what was the problem? He pointed to the first quarter's performance numbers: they were basically flat. None of the new performance improvements were showing any efficacy. With the kind of velocity the company had achieved in the fourth quarter there should have been some good carry-over into the first quarter. We should be on track for another banner year.

And we better have a banner year: our cost-savings and efficiency improvements on the supply-chain and manufacturing side, as well as the improvements in customer satisfaction by the sales team, had us poised to significantly outpace our competitors. We'd been able to absorb a materials cost increase which our competitors had passed on—now our customers were inquiring about increasing purchases. We'd already said yes; why wouldn't we? But our ability to deliver was now severely hampered by our flat performance. If it stayed flat, or even decreased, we'd have a lot of egg on our face with our customers—and our competitors.

What went wrong, the CEO asked again. How did we screw this up? Everyone in the room looked at each other. They knew the answer, but they did not want to say it. Finally, a brave soul—a lowly vice president simply said, *our management team and employees believe we are a bunch of liars and there is little reason to do more than what's minimally required for their jobs.*

There was a pause as the CEO digested what he'd heard. He looked around the table and most were simply looking down at their note pads. One of the other VP's wasn't. Is this true? he was asked by the CEO. Without hesitation he said yes.

The CEO then asked why people thought they'd been lied to. It soon became a more active dialogue and all the other initially silent participants began to add to the conversation. After a half-hour or so, the CEO said I think I now understand how we failed. I think I know what the problem was—and will be for this year also unless we make some changes and get the word out to our teams.

What the Problem Was: Money

For most of the executives tasked with assessing the situation in more detail for the CEO, the problem was money.

Our company had preached through the year about how it would reward those who excelled. They did—then the company poorly rewarded them.

There was a meeting of the committee with the CEO to provide an update on their problem identification task. They started by having the vice president of human resources, who was responsible for all facets of employee compensation, explain how the previous year had been budgeted. The CEO followed this with rapt attention.

The process was fairly simple, and had been followed to

the letter the prior fiscal year. Although the numbers were much higher, given that it was a two billion dollar company, it was presented with hypothetical numbers to make the math straight forward.

Total Planned Employee Compensation: $10,000,000

Expected Inflation Rate: 2.0%

Planned average employee wage increases: 2.5%

Dollar planned wage increases: $250,000

Actual FY Employee Compensation: $10,110,000

(The additional $110,000 was due to unbudgeted overtime when higher than planned sales orders required additional operating hours to meet customer demands.)

Actual Inflation Rate: 1.95%

New FY planned Compensation: $10, 250,000

But—to stay within the current year FY plan of $10,250,000, raises coming out of the last FY would have to be limited to $140,000: (250,000 – 110,000). Wage increases were based on an employee's actual compensation for that year—so some, by working company directed substantial overtime, had "cut in to" the amount which could be spent for the coming year's raises.

As the HR budget team calculated the impact, they could still stay at the planned total-spend not exceed to target of $10,250,000 the planning committee had committed to achieving.

This commitment had been made in the mid-year planning for the upcoming fiscal year, before the completion of the actual year's results. The actual performance exceeded net profit expectations by 12%.

Accordingly the actual target merit increase level, released to the responsible P&L executives and their management teams, was a target increase of 1.3% for those meeting expectations and 1.5% to those for exceeding expectations. Managers could reduce the target 1.3% for some individuals in order to give high performers 1.5% so long as the total change did not exceed 1.4% for that sub-organization.

By holding the various teams to this standard, the new wage projection for the upcoming year was held to a total spend of $140,000 based on the commitment not to exceed $10,250,000.

The CEO sat back, looking at the numbers. He couldn't fault the vice president of human resources or her team: they had been told no more than 2.5% year over year, and they had delivered on that. With the updates on projected overtime built into the new operating budget, given the prior year experience, that $10,250,000 number was where it was supposed to be.

The wage increase was one part of the story. The other part was the incentive program for non-executive members of the management team. There had been a lot of grumbling there as well, with members disappointed they had not received a bonus 10-12% greater than their target.

The actual numbers were used for the one hundred management team members who were eligible.

Eligible Managers: 100. Band Level: Average Salary: Target Bonus: Budget Spend

50 I $70,000 10% $350,000

35 II $85,000 15% $446,250

15 III $100,000 20% $300,000

Total: $1,096,250

Amount budgeted—anticipating normal turnover:

90% or $986,625

Total amount paid to eligible managers: $986,625

Average percentage of target paid to those who 'met performance': 85%

'Exceeded performance': 91%

The budgeted numbers had not been exceeded.

The CEO sat back and looked at that chart. *Just to be clear—in a year where we outperformed by 12% as a company, if I was a solidly performing manager or director my bonus was 85% of target, and if I exceeded performance, I received 96% of my target?*

The vice president of human resources proudly said yes, that is correct: but we ensured we didn't go over budget, she added.

And as I recall, the CEO continued, *all of our executives received at least 25%* ***more*** *than their target expectations, up to* ***100% more*** *depending on their executive position?*

He was again told, with an earnest smile, that was correct.

Of course, the year-end stock report for the company was about to be released, and the total compensation of the C-Suite executives would be included with a breakdown of their bonus compensation. All of the company's employees were shareholders to some degree. The CEO was very proud it was one of the company benefits. All would get a copy of the year-end report in the next thirty days, delivered right to their door courtesy of the U.S. postal service. The industrious employees would be reading it online a week before the mail arrived, when it was released.

The CEO's target bonus was $200,000 a year: he'd received $400,000 when the bonus checks were mailed. The other C-suite executives had received checks ranging from $220,000 to $350,000. And it was all there in the stock report. He had the advance copy of the stock report in his binder: he'd have to approve it in the next day so it could be published on time.

Everyone in the room looked at him, wondering what he was thinking. He nodded, stood, and left without saying anything else.

What the Problem *Really* Was: Money and Trust

I was told that the CEO summoned the COO to his office an hour or so later.

As to what was said, I do not know. As to what was now required, it became apparent very quickly. All of the operating divisions were to go back and revise their annual budgets, with some very different guidance.

The CEO realized that everyone had met their commitments—except for him. He had a commitment to the shareholders and to the employees at all levels and he had let the employees down. But he also knew he couldn't do some massive 180 that would undermine customer or shareholder confidence. The issue was money, yes; but the bigger issue was trust. How could he keep what he had to the external stakeholders and recover what he had lost to the internal stakeholders—his employees. He would need to redo the budget for the coming year.

To make the internal commitment a deliverable would require some bold moves. And it would require some changes within the corporation and then to his reporting structure. What he had preached would happen came nowhere close to what actually happened. He'd failed to reward the parts of the company which truly exceeded the goals

His next call was to the CFO. Apparently that meeting lasted well into the night.

What We Then Did

It took a week or so before the CFO and the COO had a plan the CEO would accept.

Then the rest of the C-suite was brought on board and told

what would be done. It wasn't a negotiation. Then the rest of the executive team was brought on board. Those with the actual P&L responsibility for the operating divisions of the company were ecstatic.

The higher-than-expected profits from the prior year had been mainly placed into the capital budget. About half of the amount had not yet been committed. That money was pulled back into the COO's operating budget. Also, the corporate HR function was moved from reporting to the CEO to reporting to the COO. While compensation execution was still under the HR group, all compensation decisions were made by the COO and CFO.

It was decided that all company employees outside of the executive group, in all functions, would receive an across-the-board wage or salary increase of an additional 3.5% effective day one of the third quarter. That would bring the annualized increase for everyone at better than 2.5%. Each manager and supervisor sat with their respective employee's and gave them that update.

For the management team members, it was calculated for each what the difference was between 115% of their prior FY target bonus and what they received. They likewise got a make-up bonus of the difference effective the beginning of the third quarter. For those who had already received a higher amount as a high performer, their adjusted amount was based on 125%.

All of this was done at the manager level, quietly and without fanfare. This was a COO initiative as approved by the CEO. The department managers and operating division executives kept it low key, a recognition of the outstanding financial performance shown by the end-of-year numbers, which were not anticipated as the current budget year's budget was finalized. And it was also pointed out that the CEO had 'made it right.'

The COO and his team, which supervised the majority of

the bonus-eligible management team members, went back and looked at how the management-bonus budget should be calculated. It was determined to fully fund the possible payout at 125%. This change was communicated to the participants across the company, and the budget target for each band was increased by an additional 2.5%.

The payout structure would be still be division based: each operating division's end-of-year performance to target would be the basis for bonus payout. If the division came in at 90%, the bonus target would be reduced to 90% for a 'meet's expectations' bonus: if it was 115%, then that would be the cutoff for a 'meets expectations' manager. It was also decided there would be no artificial limit placed upon the number of eligible managers to 'exceeds expectations,' so long as the total budgeted amount for bonuses was not exceeded for the division.

What We Did Right

When the first quarter of the next FY came the following year, the CEO and the shareholders were pleased with the final results.

The company, after the mid-year reset of the budget, still performed at 104% to a very hard target.

The lowest performing division came in at 98.8% and the best performing came in at 111% to their respective targets. The CEO used some of his discretionary funds to bring the least performing division to 100% with a cautionary note to that management team he expected them to bring in a great number for the new fiscal year.

During the fourth quarter the CEO made a number of visits to all of the key locations, conducting financial performance reviews with the management teams. He causally admitted dropping the ball at the beginning of the year relative to last year's performance, not correctly seeing in time the difference between budgeted numbers and the manner they were calculated relative to actual performance. He asked the teams how their employees had responded to the mid-year raises and the bonus corrections: he listened. He regained the trust of his management teams by actively listening and seeking their input. And he commended everyone on the performance to date, challenging each to do what they could to win.

How the Outcome Was Accepted, and Lessons Learned

My client tells me the company continued to perform well, even during the COVID-19 issues.

Morale remained high for management and employees, and the company has continued to see increasing sales and solid profitability.

The biggest lesson learned was understanding that when the foundation of trust has been eroded—fix it as quickly as possible before it is completely destroyed. The CEO of this company, with his key executives, recognized they needed to fix things: they succeeded.

Chapter Six

The Hard Part About Communications

By Dr. Mike Hackney

"I just can't do that, boss!"

How many times have you heard that from team members when it comes to speaking to others, or, even better, presenting or speaking to a group?

And how many times have you seen others get up in front of a team, a meeting, even a presentation, thinking they are doing just great, they're informative, entertaining, the best thing since sliced bread, and they are awful?

Speaking to anyone, outside of the most informal of conversations, is the most difficult thing for many to do. Even informal conversations can tie a person up in knots. And the cruel humor behind that little fact is on the television daily—all the comedy shows use the inability of someone to communicate effectively as the show's punchline or ridicule. It's all around us.

Yet, and this presumes you—the reader—are comfortable speaking to others, speaking to a group, giving a presentation, dealing with higher-up's in an organizational structure, you are in a small collection of folks. Few of us are comfortable. Many of us are game to try—but are we really that good?

Would we like to be better—and along the way take those who cannot do it very well—if at all—and help them achieve some effective skills and be more confident?

The Big Meeting

Earlier in my career I was a plant manager for a 300+ person team that made food items.

We were part of a large division that was itself part of a major corporation. Our higher-ups were all very poised, capable, polished types—some would say arrogant, a least a few of them, with little appreciation (and to this day I do not know why) for those with poor or even non-existent communications skills. And here they were for a big meeting.

A couple of those folks seemed to delight in making fun of lower ranking team members attempting to communicate information, or make a presentation on a topic. No one wanted to be the one speaking. Knowing it might be required was enough for people to feign illness to avoid the humiliation from those bosses. That put the onus on the couple of team members who were the most effective communicators to carry the team. It wasn't fair, but it was reality.

We got through the Big Meeting. But it wasn't pleasant, it wasn't particularly useful (to us) and the higher-ups went on their merry way. We were glad they were gone and already dreading their return.

I was new to the team—I'd been there a couple of weeks and was still formulating my initial assessment on what priorities for development were most needed. I'd already identified our collective communications skills as a management group needed to improve, but the team's reaction to the Big Meeting made me realize I needed to elevate that part of the team's—and key individuals'—development to a more immediate priority.

Small Steps

Before we can improve ourselves—or others—we need to develop three things: a realistic appraisal of where we are, an achievable goal of where we want to go, then a roadmap of the steps, tasks, trainings, coaching's, practices, etc., of how we can get there.

And that had to be done on two key separate levels: as a team, and by individual.

The team was lucky: we had a couple of people who had the ability—and a personal sense of ease—to speak to others in a variety of settings. The others, ranging in position from first level managers to first level directors, had lessor abilities. But all could improve.

However, there is a circumstance in any improvement action called *observation bias*. If I know someone is watching me to see if I improved, then I may or may not react in a very natural manner—and I will be self-conscious about being observed.

I needed to set up a natural requirement what could serve as a place for everyone to practice—without feeling like they were being judged while practicing.

My direct reports and I had already initiated a new format of morning meetings. Like most organizations we started each day with a meeting. Mine was a three-part presentation by each of the management team members. And if they couldn't make the meeting, their department needed to be represented by the next person in their chain of command. The three parts were a brief overview of how their department had performed the previous workday to the key performance indicators we tracked as a team; what were the key activities affecting their team for today, and—as they listened to the other managers give their reports, what could they do to help? Naturally the first and second persons speaking would have to jump in as others spoke after them if there was an area where they could contribute.

That "how-to-do-this-morning-meeting-effectively" will be the subject of a future chapter. But I added a new wrinkle. On a rotating basis each manager would have to give an update on how the facility as a whole was performing—to that day—for the current reporting period. This addressed two issues: first, a general lack of knowledge as to how we were achieving goals that affected our "Corporate Scorecard" for each four-week reporting period, and it caused tomorrow's reporting manager to solicit updates from his peer group during the coming day.

Now that may sound simple enough—but it was such a deviation from the former status quo (isn't knowing all of that just the plant manager's job?) to compelling one-to-one interaction between silos.

Because I *did* know what was going on. I needed all of them to take on a larger sense of ownership for working together, not just handling what each had decided was 'their' job, versus the overall performance of the plant. Again—that will also be the subject of another future chapter.

But what it additionally did, was force each of them to present to the team. At least one to two times every three weeks. And it wasn't an off-the-cuff presentation. It was brief, but it followed yesterdays from someone else and theirs would be followed by someone else tomorrow. If you are thinking collaboration and improvement in teamwork, those would be a big yes. But for this task at hand I was also interested in improving presentation skills. We still had a long way to go.

Bigger Steps

In medical training, they are real big on 'see one, do one, teach one.'

A patient with a bad laceration across their arm needs to have it cleaned, examined for extent of injuries, perhaps a few stitches, then bandaged and initial post treatment care, like an antibiotic or painkiller prescription if needed (which only the licensed docs actually do.)

The student—who could be virtually anyone at any level training for patient care, from a paramedic to a medical student, watches how a pro does it. Then, when the next patient comes in, that student does it (under supervision.) But here is the real joy: substantial research has shown that after doing it a couple of times themselves, when the student is tasked to teach *another* how to do it—not only is the 'how to' reinforced and the student gets better at doing it—they also get better at understanding it because they are seeing someone else's mistakes and it is up to them to correct them.

With this in mind I tasked each department head to give me three briefings during each reporting period. The first was on what their team was going to do to be better as a department and support all the others. The one in the middle of the period was a progress report on where they were and how they were doing to their prior commitments. The final one was as at the end of the period on how had they actually done compared to their previous commitments. But I threw in a caveat: I didn't want to hear it from the department head. I wanted to hear it from one of his/her direct reports—and not the same one each time.

It's human nature to want to avoid looking bad in front of a boss. This meant the department head had to coach and develop the team members on how to do the presentations—and they all had to help each other.

Care to guess what happened to the department head's communication skills?

Being a Starter

In sports there are those who start, those who get in the game a good bit as a substitute, and the proverbial bench warmers.

The job of the coach—me, you—is to help each person at each level improve. Not everyone will be a star, but many—most—can get better. And the improvement isn't always obvious because it isn't just about the individual's capabilities, it is how it affects the entire team. In organizational improvement, this team effect is the most critical because it enhances the total organization. But teams are made up of individuals—and most of us want to be a starter. Most of us want to be seen for the contribution we are confidently making.

As the department heads improved their public speaking skills with each daily meeting to the senior management team, they also improved as they found themselves coaching their managers and supervisors on those same skills. Several, not all, of the department heads began insisting their direct reports have supervisors and hourly employees train on how to brief them—or me as the plant manager—on what was going on whenever one of us walked into the area.

Everyone, mostly—there is always the curmudgeon—now wanted to be the starter. It was about pride. It was about confidence that they knew what was being asked—and they were confident in how to present it. And confidence is contagious. Also—it impacts everyone's wallet: the better we performed, the higher the employee bonus payouts we did quarterly. No one was sad to get bigger paychecks.

And for the management team—that changed a lot as well over the next year, a little bit at a time, each incremental improvement serving as the foundation for the next one. I now did a lot less talking and a lot more listening at our daily and weekly business meetings as the department heads confidently and knowledgeably briefed me and the rest of the team on where their department was, where it was going—and how they were assisting the other departments of the plant. I had questions, they had answers. They ran their singular responsibilities as part of a collaborative team, and the better they got, the better we got.

The Super Bowl

It had been a year since the higher-ups had last visited us as they made their trek across the corporation, away from their corporate luxuries and conveniences, heading out to where the products were actually made.

A couple of the more arrogant ones were still doing what they'd always done, and they came along for the trip, but this time no one was calling in sick to avoid their insults.

Visits from the higher ups always had three main parts. First, after the greetings, there was a briefing from the plant manager to the higher up and his entourage while the senior management team watched and maybe assisted with questions. Next, there would be a walk through the facility and its various parts, led by the plant manager with the CEO or COO or whomever the higher up was doing the visit, while the other bosses and entourage tagged along. Last, there was a final meeting, usually in the plant manager's office: the direct chain of command, led by the Big Boss, would tell the plant manager their disappointments from the visit, the year, and chastise the plant manager about his sins. This method, cast in stone from time immortal was *NOT* to be changed.

But not this Super Bowl. The plant had performed well on all metrics over the last year, and the formal briefing began in our conference room. But it went differently. I sat in my chair, facilitated the agenda, and otherwise said little if anything; each department head gave excellent reports on their areas, and even the couple of "I'm so smart" higher-ups had little to say.

When we went on the tour I introduced the senior higher-up to one of our hourly employees—who walked beside the Big Boss around the facility, answering all his questions. I stayed back with my boss, raising some eyebrows from the entourage. At each key area of the plant, and for each support department, two or three hourlies and supervisors handled the walk-throughs of their areas while their bosses stood by. And watched.

The meeting in the plant manager's office when it was all over lasted maybe five minutes. Partly because the big boss asked so many questions on the tour, as he was completely enthralled with how effectively the team members were representing their areas, that they were now an hour off schedule. And partly because he wasn't sure what to say. I was fine with that. So was my team.

The Ability to Communicate is Key

This short chapter does not do justice to the books written about teaching managers how to communicate effectively: it is not easy, but it is doable, and can be effectively and subliminally interwoven into the daily routine.

There are many reasons why someone has difficulties communicating, or desires not to even try; and not everyone is going to become a great public speaker. But almost everyone can become better. It simply takes a mechanism that compels them to interact, that offers the time and coaching to improve.

The three major takeaways from my own experiences at differing companies investing in improving communications capabilities are these:

1. Although it takes time, the more **confident** I am (at any level) at communicating, the more confident *team members* will become; particularly if I require them to also practice and **refine their own** communication skills.

2. The better the *total team* can **communicate at all levels**, the more money everyone makes, the less stress everyone endures, and the arrogant higher-ups seek easier targets (always a bonus.)

3. **Increased levels** of communication breaks down silos, increases teamwork within teams, and *collaboration between different areas* of the organization: everyone may not be a starter—but **everyone is key** to the *winning team*.

Please let me know how you've improved communications skills on your team, or if your team could benefit from becoming better at communicating between themselves, and with other stakeholders to your organization.

Chapter Seven

Stepping Back to Lead Forward: Leadership Lessons from the Trenches of Event Production

By Robert Grossman

The Ultimate Leadership Test

Have you ever found yourself clinging to control when everything inside you screamed that you should be the one in charge? I certainly did. After years of building my meeting production company, Focus Creative Group, I was transitioning to a new venture—Black Diamond Leadership—focused on developing high-performance leaders and teams. As I was making this shift, an unexpected opportunity arose that would test everything I planned to teach others.

A long-time client called to request that I produce their division's annual summit for Deloitte. What started as a relatively straightforward meeting quickly evolved into one of the most complex events I'd ever undertaken. The scope expanded dramatically, transforming from an $80,000 production to a $700,000 extravaganza at the Wynn Hotel in Las Vegas. This expansion wasn't just in budget—it was in complexity, spectacle, and team size.

As I prepared to launch a company centered on high-performance leadership principles, the universe handed me the perfect laboratory. This project would force me to practice what I was preparing to preach, requiring me to apply emotional intelligence principles in real time under significant pressure. Little did I know that the greatest leadership lessons would come not from what I did but from what I learned to stop doing.

Building the Dream Team

My first challenge emerged before we even arrived on site. As the project's scope expanded, I quickly realized I couldn't handle it alone. In a moment of self-awareness (or perhaps desperation), I approached my creative director, Dean, for guidance. His advice was simple yet revolutionary for someone accustomed to maintaining tight control: "Let me hire the lead team members we'll need."

This was my first breakthrough moment—allowing someone else to build the core team. Dean recommended three key people: one for technical production, another for creative production (set design, lighting, special effects), and a third to lead media development for presentations and videos. Instead of personally vetting and hiring each team member, I took a deep breath and empowered Dean to assemble the best talent he knew.

Dean's team was exceptional, but this meant working with industry professionals I hadn't personally selected. These were experts at the top of their game, accustomed to producing events even larger than ours. My role was shifting before my eyes, transitioning from hands-on producer to executive leader—a position that would require a completely different approach than what had built my success to date.

As pre-production progressed, the excitement built around our "No Limits" theme. The opening would feature Cirque du Soleil performers emerging from giant boxes on stage, followed by a surprise reveal when they were replaced by the meeting leaders in matching costumes. It would culminate in pyrotechnics as the CEO made his entrance. On paper, it was spectacular—ambitious, memorable, and perfectly aligned with the theme. In reality, it would become my master class in high-performance leadership.

The Leadership Identity Crisis

The first day on-site delivered my first significant test. After arriving at the Wynn, I met with Ed, my technical director, to discuss the morning's load-in schedule. "I'll see you tomorrow at 5 AM for load-in," I stated confidently, following my usual protocol. His response caught me off guard: "You don't need to be here for that. You can show up around 11 o'clock."

At that moment, I felt my pulse quicken as a wave of anxiety washed over me. Who was I, if not the first person on-site and the last to leave? What would my client think if I wasn't visibly directing every aspect of the setup? My identity as a leader was being challenged, triggering an emotional response that threatened to override my rational thinking.

This was a classic "key moment" in emotional intelligence—a triggering event that could prompt a reactive or thoughtful response. As I felt the familiar surge of defensive energy, I recognized it for what it was: my ego feeling threatened. Drawing on the principles I planned to teach, I stepped back mentally and responded simply, "Great, I'll see you at 11."

That night was excruciating. I paced my hotel room, checked my phone obsessively, and arrived outside the ballroom at 10:45 AM, wearing a path in the carpet before finally entering at 11:00. What I saw inside stunned me. Approximately 50 people efficiently set up the room—riggers on lifts running cables across the ceiling, technicians building the stage, and the core team directing it all with precision.

After briefly introducing the crew, Ed delivered another unexpected blow: "Why don't you come back around four o'clock? Go back to your room and sell the next project." Again, I felt that familiar pang of irrelevance but managed to smile and walk away. Little did I realize my team was teaching me how to be the leader they needed.

The Empty Chair

When I returned at four o'clock, the ballroom had transformed. Most of the crew had completed their tasks, leaving only the core team to make final adjustments. As I made my way to the technical riser at the back of the room—my usual command post—I encountered my second profound leadership moment: there was no chair for me.

I had directed events from this position for years, calling cues and managing the technical flow. Now, I was expected to be somewhere else. My heart raced as I approached Dean, fighting to keep my voice even. "Where am I supposed to sit?" I asked, trying to mask my discomfort.

His response was simple but transformative: "You're not sitting up here. You should go sit with your client. You can constantly get feedback from your client and relay that to us." My immediate thought was that my client would question my value if I wasn't visibly working—running around, solving problems, directing traffic. How could I justify my role if I wasn't in the middle of everything?

That's when a crucial realization hit me: my client hadn't hired me to personally run every aspect of the production. They hired me to deliver an exceptional event, which meant assembling and leading the best possible team. My value wasn't in controlling every detail but creating the conditions for excellence to emerge.

This mental shift didn't come easily. It required acknowledging that my leadership identity had been too wrapped up in being needed for every decision. True leadership meant building a team that could function brilliantly without my constant intervention—perhaps even better than when I micromanaged every detail.

"You're Not a Jerk"

As preparations continued, I wandered the ballroom with an unfamiliar sense of spaciousness—observing rather than directing. During one of these walks, the audio director,

Bruce, called me over. "I want to let you know that you're not a jerk," he said matter-of-factly.

Taken aback, I asked what he meant. His explanation was illuminating: "People usually in your position, Executive Producer, run around, bark orders, get in the middle of everything, break down communication, and don't let the teamwork. You're the exact opposite. When we had a conflict between audio and video, you stepped in, reminded us of our core values and how we needed to communicate, and then stepped out and let us solve the problem ourselves. I've never experienced that before."

This unsolicited feedback revealed something profound: my discomfort with stepping back was creating space for others to step forward. The team wasn't interpreting my new approach as a weakness—they saw it as a strength. By allowing experts to do what they did best without micromanagement, I was enabling a level of collaboration that wouldn't have been possible under my previous leadership style.

Throughout the setup days, I continued to manage my instincts to jump in and take over. Each time I felt that urge, I recognized it as a "key moment" requiring emotional intelligence rather than reactive behavior. Gradually, I settled into my new role as the bridge between my team and the client—a position that allowed me to add value in ways I never could have while trying to control every detail.

When the Pyro Doesn't Fire

Then came the moment of truth—the opening of the meeting. Eight hundred attendees entered a darkened room with subtle lighting and meditative music—a deliberately subdued atmosphere designed to build toward a dramatic reveal. As planned, Cirque du Soleil performers emerged from boxes on stage, performed briefly, then disappeared behind the boxes for the secret switch. The three meeting leaders appeared in matching costumes, removing them to reveal themselves before building to a crescendo announcing the

"No Limits" theme

Everything was perfectly executed until the final moment—when the pyrotechnics were supposed to explode as the CEO emerged. The pyro didn't fire. The box opened, and the CEO walked out, but the dramatic explosion that would have punctuated the theme failed to materialize.

From the back of the room, I watched in horror, immediately thinking, "You blew it. You stepped out on the skinny branches and failed spectacularly. Bill (the client) is going to be furious." The old me would have stormed backstage, looking for someone to blame and trying to personally fix everything.

Instead, I stayed in position until the CEO finished his remarks, then walked (not stormed) backstage. Before I could say a word, I noticed my four lead team members huddled together intensely. Dean turned to me and said, "Robert, okay, the pyro didn't work. But we've come up with a whole new ending."

In the thirty minutes since the malfunction, they had devised an entirely new closing sequence for the three-day meeting. They would rebuild the boxes that were supposed to explode, stencil them with the limiting beliefs discussed throughout the conference, and have the CEO return with a cartoon-style dynamite plunger to symbolically blow up these limitations at the meeting's conclusion.

As they shared their solution, we were interrupted—the meeting had broken for a break, and Bill was headed straight for me, clearly looking for an explanation about the failed pyrotechnics. "Robert, what the hell happened to my pyro?" he demanded, his frustration evident.

The old me would have apologized profusely, promised to fix it, and possibly thrown someone under the bus. Instead, I replied, "Bill, I know it didn't work, and sometimes that happens with live events. But I want you to hear what my team has developed as an alternative ending." I turned to Dean and invited him to share their solution.

At that moment, I realized something crucial—that attributing the solution to my team didn't diminish my leadership; it strengthened it. Bill's eyes lit up as he heard the new plan. "This is brilliant," he exclaimed. "We literally could not have created a better ending for this meeting."

The Transformed Leader

The remaining three days of the conference unfolded with the smoothness of true teamwork. Yes, we faced challenges—live events always present unexpected difficulties—but our collaborative approach meant problems were solved quickly and creatively, often without the client or attendees ever knowing they existed.

My role had transformed completely. Instead of racing around putting out fires, I sat with my client during sessions, gathering feedback and insights that I could share with my team during breaks. I became the bridge between the client's vision and my team's execution—a role far more valuable than trying to be the solution to every problem.

The audience erupted in applause when the meeting concluded with the CEO dramatically "blowing up" the boxes of limitations. What had begun as a technical failure had become the perfect metaphor for the "No Limits" theme—demonstrating our ability to overcome obstacles through creativity and collaboration.

As we packed up after the event, I reflected on how profoundly my understanding of leadership had changed in just a few days. I had arrived in Las Vegas believing I was there to apply my leadership philosophy. Instead, I had received a master class in what high-performance leadership truly means.

Leadership Lessons From the Empty Chair

The most powerful insight from this experience was counterintuitive: sometimes, the best thing a leader can do is get out of the way. By removing myself from the center of every decision, I created space for my team's expertise and creativity to flourish. This wasn't abandonment—empowerment built on careful selection of capable team members and clear communication of values and objectives.

I learned that leadership identity can become a trap when it's too wrapped up in being needed. The shift from "I am valuable because I solve all problems" to "I am valuable because I build teams that solve problems effectively" represents a crucial evolution for any leader seeking to scale their impact. This requires emotional intelligence to recognize and manage the discomfort of letting go of control.

Perhaps most importantly, I discovered that attribution is the highest form of leadership. When I openly acknowledged that the brilliant solution came from my team rather than claiming it as my own, I didn't appear weak—I demonstrated confidence in my leadership approach. This transparency-built trust with my team and client, creating a foundation for authentic collaboration.

Applying These Lessons Beyond Event Production

These principles extend far beyond the world of event production. In any leadership context—whether managing a department, leading a project team, or running an entire organization—the temptation to micromanage is powerful. We often believe our success depends on our personal involvement in every decision, but this approach creates bottlenecks and stifles our teams' potential.

True high-performance leadership requires intentionally creating space for others to contribute their expertise. This means carefully selecting team members with complementary skills, clearly communicating values and objectives, and then having the courage to step back. It means managing your emotional responses when your leadership identity feels threatened, recognizing these as opportunities for growth rather than signs of diminishment.

This evolution can be particularly challenging for leaders

transitioning from hands-on management to executive leadership. The skills that made you successful in operational roles—attention to detail, technical expertise, and personal problem—solving—may actually hinder your effectiveness at higher levels. Embracing the discomfort of letting go is essential for scaling your impact.

The ultimate measure of your leadership isn't what you personally accomplish—it's what your team accomplishes because of the environment you create. When you build a culture where people feel empowered to contribute their best ideas and take ownership of solutions, you multiply your impact exponentially.

Following this experience, I launched Black Diamond Leadership, and these lessons became the cornerstone of my approach to developing high-performance leaders. The empty chair at the technical riser taught me more about leadership than any book or theory ever could—sometimes, the most powerful place for a leader to sit is not at the center of the action but alongside those they serve.

Chapter Eight

The Safety to Soar: How Psychological Safety Transforms Teams and Organizations

By Robert Grossman

Facing the Safety Paradox

"Robert, we have a problem." The voice on the other end of the phone belonged to a senior director at a large corporation. "Our safety and compliance department is struggling—the team responsible for keeping everyone safe is dysfunctional. Ironic, isn't it?"

As the director continued, a familiar pattern emerged. Turnover was increasing, communication breakdowns were frequent, and, most troubling, incidents and near-misses weren't being reported promptly because team members feared negative consequences.

"We've tried everything," the director sighed. "New procedures, team-building exercises, even reorganizing the department. Nothing's working."

"Let me ask you something," I said. "Do your team members feel safe speaking up when they see a problem or have a different perspective?"

There was a long pause. "Probably not. But isn't that just workplace politics? Every organization has that."

This response highlights a critical paradox: the teams responsible for managing risk often operate in environments where interpersonal risk-taking feels dangerous. Team members responsible for identifying problems hesitate to point them out—especially when those problems involve leadership decisions or established practices.

"What you're describing," I explained, "is a lack of psychological safety—the shared belief that the team is safe for interpersonal risk-taking. Without it, people hide concerns, withhold ideas, and cover up mistakes."

The director shared some remarkable news six months after implementing our psychological safety framework. "Our incident reporting is up, but actual incidents are down. People are speaking up earlier, and we're catching problems before they become serious. My leadership team asked what changed in our department."

What changed was psychological safety—and it transformed how this team functioned at every level.

This chapter tells the story of how we did it—and how you can do the same.

Understanding Psychological Safety

Psychological safety is the shared understanding that team members won't be punished or humiliated for sharing ideas, questions, concerns, or mistakes. It's a team climate characterized by interpersonal trust and mutual respect—an environment where people are comfortable being themselves.

Harvard Business School professor Amy Edmondson's groundbreaking research, which spans more than a decade, has established psychological safety as a critical component of high-performing teams. In fact, Google's comprehensive two-year study (Project Aristotle) found that psychological safety was the most important factor in determining team success—more important than individual talent, experience, or even leadership.

Why is this the case? In today's VUCA world (Volatile, Uncertain, Complex, and Ambiguous), teams face unprecedented challenges: • Disruptive innovation occurring at dizzying rates • Social media accelerates the spread of information • Increasing complexity requiring cross-functional collaboration • Remote and hybrid work environments create new communication challenges

In such conditions, organizations can't afford to have employees who are afraid to speak up. They need everyone's ideas, observations, and concerns to navigate successfully. Yet psychological safety remains rare. One study found that 85% of employees feel unable to raise concerns with their bosses, and 74% withhold ideas for improvement.

When I work with organizations to develop psychological safety, I focus on what I call the "Leadership Power Quadrant":

1. **Emotional Mastery**: Leaders who understand and manage their emotions create the foundation for psychological safety. When leaders react angrily or defensively to challenging information, they shut down communication instantly.

2. **Communication**: Clear, open communication creates the pathways to psychological safety. This includes both speaking with candor and listening with empathy.

3. **Trust**: Trust is both an input and an output of psychological safety. Leaders build trust by demonstrating competence, reliability, honesty, and genuine care for team members.

4. **Shared Responsibility**: Psychological safety flourishes when everyone understands they have the right and the responsibility to contribute to the team's success.

In the case of the safety team I mentioned earlier, all four elements were compromised. Leaders were reacting emotionally to bad news, communication channels were clogged with fear, trust had eroded, and team members had retreated into silos of individual responsibility. The transformation began by measuring exactly where they stood.

Measuring What Matters

"You can't improve what you don't measure." This business axiom is particularly true for something as intangible yet impactful as psychological safety. As one of the first U.S. graduates certified by the Fearless Organization to implement Professor Edmondson's assessment tools, I've found that measuring psychological safety provides both a crucial baseline and a powerful wake-up call for teams.

The Psychological Safety Scan measures and improves psychological safety within teams and organizations. It provides insights across four key domains:

1. **Willingness to Help**: Measures how readily team members support each other
2. **Inclusion & Diversity**: Assesses the degree of openness to diverse perspectives and inclusion of all team members
3. **Attitude to Risk & Failure**: Evaluates the team's comfort with taking risks and learning from mistakes
4. **Open Conversation**: Measures the ability of team members to discuss challenges and ideas freely

When I introduced the Psychological Safety Scan to the safety team, the results revealed significant opportunities for improvement. While I maintain confidentiality around specific client data, this team—like many I've worked with—showed particular weakness in the "Attitude to Risk & Failure" domain. Team members consistently reported feeling that mistakes would be held against them and that taking risks would lead to punishment.

The assessment also revealed something equally important: inconsistent experiences across the team. Some members felt relatively safe, while others felt extremely vulnerable, creating an unpredictable environment where people couldn't be sure how their ideas or concerns would be received.

However, the power of measurement goes beyond numbers. The assessment process sent a message: leadership cared enough about the team environment to measure it. The director later told me, "Just asking these questions started conversations we'd never had before."

It's important to note that measuring psychological safety isn't about proving the workplace is safe—it's about identifying areas that need improvement. I clarified to the team that we wanted honest responses and that leadership would address the issues they revealed, not target those who provided negative feedback.

With a clear understanding of where the team stood, we could begin the real work of transformation.

Creating the Conditions for Psychological Safety

The next morning, I gathered the team's leadership for a crucial conversation. "The good news," I told them, "is that you now know where you stand. The better news is that psychological safety can be improved systematically."

We began with leadership because psychological safety cascades from the top. Leaders create the conditions through their behaviors, not their intentions or pronouncements. The safety team leaders committed to four specific actions:

1. **Frame the work as learning, not execution.** The department had fallen into a performance mindset where mistakes were unacceptable. We reframed their work as continuous learning, where mistakes were valuable data points. When a safety incident report was filed incorrectly, instead of

asking, "Who messed this up?" the new approach was, "What can we learn from this to improve our process?"

2. Acknowledge fallibility. The director began modeling vulnerability by openly admitting when he didn't have all the answers. "I don't know yet, but let's figure it out together" became a powerful phrase that permitted others to acknowledge their uncertainties.

3. Model curiosity. Leaders committed to asking more questions and making fewer statements. Simple queries like "What might we be missing here?" and "What alternative approaches should we consider?" invited diverse perspectives. One manager transformed her team meetings by shifting from mostly talking to actively listening and asking questions, resulting in greater participation and surfacing issues that would have otherwise remained hidden.

4. Embrace productive conflict. We distinguished between relationship conflict (personal, emotional, damaging) and task conflict (focused on ideas, productive, and necessary). Through role-playing exercises, leaders practiced facilitating disagreements about ideas while maintaining respect for people.

With leadership setting the tone, we expanded our focus to the entire team through a series of workshops and coaching sessions targeting each element of the Leadership Power Quadrant:

Emotional Mastery We introduced practical techniques for managing emotional triggers: • The "key moment pause"-taking a breath before responding to triggering events • Emotion labeling—naming feelings to reduce their power • Perspective-taking exercises to see situations through others' eyes.

One team lead shared how this transformed her approach: "I used to react immediately when someone questioned my safety protocols. Now, I pause, acknowledge my defensive feeling, and respond with curiosity instead. The conversations are completely different."

Communication We established new communication norms: • "No interruption" rules during brainstorming • Structured turn-taking in meetings to ensure all voices were heard • "What I heard you say..." confirmation practices to improve understanding • Regular anonymous feedback channels for sensitive issues

Trust Trust-building activities focused on consistency and follow-through: • Leaders committed to "closing the loop" on all suggestions • Team agreements about confidentiality were established • Recognition practices highlighted contributions from all team members • Transparency about decision-making processes became standard

Shared Responsibility To break down silos and create collective ownership: • Cross-training increased understanding of different roles • Decision authority was pushed downward where appropriate • Collective problem-solving sessions replaced top-down directives • Success metrics became team-based rather than individual

Throughout this process, resistance was inevitable. Some team members viewed psychological safety as "soft" or unnecessary, while others feared it would lower standards or accountability. We addressed these concerns directly, emphasizing that psychological safety isn't about lowering expectations—it's about creating conditions where people can meet higher expectations through collaboration, innovation, and learning.

As one skeptical safety officer told me later, "I thought this was just another corporate program. But when I saw my manager change how she responded to problems, I realized this approach was different."

The Psychological Safety Transformation

Signs of transformation emerged three months into our work with the safety team. Six months in, the changes were undeniable.

A follow-up Psychological Safety Scan showed significant improvement across all four domains. While I don't share specific client data, this team's improvement exceeded typical gains I've observed in comparable engagements. Most notably, their progress in the "Attitude to Risk & Failure" domain—initially their weakest area—demonstrated how effectively they had embraced a learning-oriented culture.

But even more important than the assessment scores were the tangible changes in team behavior and performance:

Increased reporting of potential safety issues. In the past, employees hesitated to report minor issues for fear of being blamed. Now, with psychological safety established, team members report near-misses substantially more often, allowing the team to address potential problems before they become serious incidents.

Improved process innovation. A safety technician who had previously kept quiet about a cumbersome reporting procedure devised a streamlined alternative. His innovation reduced processing time significantly and was subsequently adopted company-wide.

Enhanced cross-functional collaboration. The safety team began partnering more effectively with operations, engineering, and human resources. Joint problem-solving sessions that previously devolved into finger-pointing became productive exchanges of ideas.

Reduced turnover. Before our work began, the department struggled with retention. In the months following our psychological safety initiative, significantly fewer team members voluntarily left, and several specifically mentioned the improved team climate in their stay interviews.

Leadership recognition. As mentioned at the beginning of this chapter, senior leadership noticed the department's performance improvement and specifically commended the director for the positive change.

Perhaps most telling was a comment from a veteran safety specialist: "For the first time in my career, I feel like my expertise is truly valued. I'm not just checking boxes but helping shape how we approach safety."

The director summarized the transformation: "We always possessed technical competence. What we lacked was the psychological safety to leverage that competence fully. Now, people bring their whole selves to work—their knowledge, creativity, concerns, and solutions. The difference is remarkable."

Lessons for Leaders

My experience with this safety team reflects patterns I've observed across dozens of organizations implementing psychological safety measures. Here are the key lessons for leaders who want to create this transformative environment:

Start with yourself. Psychological safety begins with your behavior as a leader. Your reactions to bad news, mistakes, and challenging ideas set the tone for your team. Develop your emotional mastery so you can respond thoughtfully rather than react impulsively.

Measure before intervening. Use a validated assessment tool to establish a baseline of psychological safety in your team. The data will guide your interventions and provide a benchmark for measuring improvement.

Be patient but persistent. Psychological safety doesn't develop overnight, especially if trust has been damaged. Be consistent in your new behaviors and recognize that team members may test the waters cautiously before fully embracing psychological safety.

Distinguish psychological safety from other concepts. Psychological safety is not about being nice, lowering standards, or avoiding conflict. It enables higher standards and productive conflict because people can speak honestly without fear.

Connect safety to outcomes. Help your team understand how psychological safety directly contributes to the results they care about—quality, innovation, efficiency, and growth. This isn't a "soft" initiative; it's a performance imperative.

Look for small wins. Celebrate instances where psychological safety leads to positive outcomes—when someone speaks up and prevents a problem or when a frank discussion leads to a better solution. These stories reinforce the value of psychological safety.

Make it systematic. Build psychological safety into your regular processes—make it part of how meetings are run, decisions are made, feedback is given, and conflicts are resolved.

Beware of regression. Under pressure, teams often revert to old patterns. During high-stress periods, be especially attentive to maintaining psychological safety when it's most needed and vulnerable.

Start Today:
Building Psychological Safety Through Curiosity

One of the most powerful ways to build psychological safety is by modeling curiosity as a leader. Instead of making statements or jumping to conclusions, ask genuine questions that invite diverse perspectives: • "What might we be missing here?" • "What alternative approaches should we consider?" • "What concerns do you have that we haven't addressed?"

When leaders demonstrate curiosity, they signal that different viewpoints are valued and that the team's collective intelligence is greater than any individual's knowledge. One manager I worked with found that by shifting from mostly talking to primarily asking questions in team meetings, participation increased dramatically and previously hidden issues surfaced in time to address them.

As I mentioned earlier, this curiosity-focused approach in the safety department led to increased reporting of potential issues because people no longer feared blame. As team members brought forward concerns earlier, actual incidents decreased, and senior leadership noticed the improvement.

The Buffalo Principle

When discussing psychological safety with leaders, I often share what author and thought leader Rory Vaden calls "the buffalo principle." When storms approach the plains, most animals run away, extending their time in the storm. Buffalo, however, run directly into the storm, minimizing their time in discomfort.

Psychological safety enables teams to be like buffalo—to face challenges directly rather than avoiding them. With psychological safety, teams can approach difficult conversations, acknowledge mistakes, challenge assumptions, and propose bold ideas. Without it, they waste energy avoiding these essential activities, prolonging their time in the "storm."

Storms are inevitable in today's business environment. Competition, technological disruption, economic uncertainty, and global crises will continue to challenge organizations. The question isn't whether your team will face storms but how they'll approach them. Will they run away, extending their discomfort? Or will they charge forward together, minimizing the pain and emerging stronger?

In the words of the safety director: "We used to waste so much energy avoiding difficult conversations and hiding problems. Now, we point them out, discuss them openly, and solve them together. It's more effective and creates a better way to work."

Creating psychological safety gives your team the confidence to be like the buffalo—to face challenges directly. It also enables teams to learn continuously and innovate fearlessly. The storm will pass faster, and your team will be stronger for facing it head-on.

Chapter Nine

The Power of Clarity: Transforming Chaos into Success

By Ski Swiatkowski

As you navigate in today's pressure-filled, highly competitive environment, here's a question to which leaders need to give serious thought. "What if the greatest obstacle to your organization's success isn't lack of effort, but lack of clarity?"

Imagine a workplace where employees show up each day uncertain about their roles, confused by mixed messages, and frustrated by a lack of direction. In such an environment, productivity suffers, morale plummets, and innovation stalls. The costs are enormous—both financially and culturally—and yet, much of this goes unnoticed. Worse yet, the root cause often goes unrecognized.

During my 40 years as a manager, executive, and management consultant, I've discovered that one of the main problems plaguing organizations large and small is lack of clarity. It is an insidious issue that can wreak havoc and lead to numerous other problems.

The Situation

Several years ago, I was hired to consult with a mortgage company that will serve as an excellent example.

Horizon Mortgage Lending (not the real name of the company), a mid-sized mortgage company which was owned by a larger organization, was in turmoil. While this example discusses a company in the mortgage industry, I believe you will see that their core problem can be found in companies in every industry.

In the year prior to my engagement with this company, the mortgage market was extremely strong. Loan origination volume (sales) for the company was soaring. People on the sales teams found it easy to generate a large number of loans without much effort. Management had a push, push, push mindset. Their unstated message was, "let's take advantage of this market by making as much money as we can, right now."

Additionally, salespeople and support staff were being hired at a frantic pace, paying them inflated salaries and high commissions just to increase capacity and loan sales volume. The company's profitability was fantastic.

Unfortunately, as is often the case, high sales volume can mask many organizational problems. This was exactly the situation with Horizon Mortgage. The new team members they hired were thrown into a hectic workplace environment. The only focus was on closing more loans. Stress levels throughout the company were through the roof.

Then, it happened. The Federal Reserve began to increase the Fed Funds Rate. The result was a market shift that sent mortgage interest rates climbing as well. As the mortgage interest rates rose, loan production began to drop. What had been an easy money market was beginning to show signs of tightening.

As the revenue dropped, staff reductions were made. Employees came to work with the fear they might be next. As you would expect, morale was low. Turnover was high. And productivity was declining. Seemingly unsure of what to do, leadership struggled to effectively engage the workforce.

As I began working with this mortgage company, I listened to frustrated managers, disengaged employees, and dissatisfied customers. I recognized the signs of dysfunction immediately. While company leadership did recognize the impact that rising interest rates had on their business, they maintained the same strategy of pressuring their sales teams for more business and looking for more experienced loan officers to bring onto the sales team.

They blamed the employees, viewing the problem as a lack of effort and accountability. The message to the salespeople was *you need to take ownership of your lack of loan production.* "Work harder!" To management, working harder was the simple solution; but it was clear to me something deeper was at play.

Identifying the Real Problem

After conducting employee surveys and leadership interviews, I was able to uncover the core issue: a lack of clarity in many areas.

In this contracting market, employees were confused about their roles, expectations, and what they could do to contribute to the company's success. Managers, in turn, struggled to provide clear direction because they were unclear as well, leading to additional frustration and disengagement. The organization lacked a unifying vision in the face of this slowing market and a consistent communication strategy that could carry them through difficult times.

Without clarity, employees felt like cogs in a machine or light bulbs that could be easily replaced rather than valuable contributors. This misalignment bred inefficiency, eroded trust, and stifled innovative thinking. The issue wasn't accountability—it was the absence of clear leadership.

The Solution: Creating a Culture of Clarity

To address the problem, I guided them through a five-phase approach:

1. **Define and Communicate a Clear Vision and Core Values** - Using input from all stakeholders, the management team worked to articulate a compelling vision and the core values that would guide the company. The vision and core values were shared through town halls, newsletters, and team meetings. This ensured that every employee understood the company's vision of the future, how the values would give them guidance and how their roles would contribute to company objectives.

2. **Conduct a SWOT Analysis** - Again, the management team guided by information from their people, identified the strengths and weaknesses within the company, as well as, the opportunities and threats they saw in the marketplace.

3. **Define the Mission** - Leveraging information from the SWOT Analysis, the management team mapped out what needed to be done in the next 12 months to stabilize consistent loan production, realizing that it would take a focused effort and time to navigate the challenges of a higher interest rate market.

4. **Establish Clear Expectations** - Based on the new mission, managers were trained to set specific, measurable, achievable, relevant, and time-bound (SMART) goals for their teams. They set up and implemented a structured feedback loop where employees received regular performance updates and guidance.

5. **Strengthen Leadership Communication** - The managers were also provided leadership training focused on aspects of emotional intelligence such as active listening and clear communication, as well as coaching techniques they could apply to their

teams. Managers were encouraged to have one-on-one check-ins with employees regularly to reinforce expectations, and provide ongoing guidance and support on new loan origination strategies.

Expanding the Framework: Building Sustainable Leadership Practices

To ensure lasting change, I worked with managers to implement additional strategies:

Empowering Employees - Beyond clarifying employee roles, the company began to foster a culture where employees were encouraged to voice ideas, share feedback, and contribute to decision-making. This effort was well received and cultivated a sense of ownership and engagement.

Aligning Leadership at All Levels - A leadership communication framework was introduced, ensuring that clear information flowed from senior executives down to frontline managers and employees. By first aligning every level of leadership and insisting on clarity, the organization began to maintain consistent messaging and company direction.

Tracking and Adjusting - We worked on implementing key performance indicators (KPIs) to measure engagement, retention, and productivity. Regular reviews allowed the leadership team to adjust strategies as needed, ensuring continuous improvement.

The Outcome: Transformation Through Clarity

And what results did they see? Within a year, even though the interest rates remained elevated, employee engagement survey scores increased by 35%, turnover dropped by 50%, and productivity surged as the culture began to take on a safer feeling for the employees.

Customer and referral partner (Realtors) satisfaction ratings improved as employees became more invested in using new strategies, technology and delivering quality service. Managers reported feeling more equipped to lead, and employees expressed greater job satisfaction and connection to their work. Clearly they were in a much better position to deal with market changes or whatever challenges they would face.

Brain Science Shows That Clear Leadership Works Better

Here is the underlying neurological challenge. When workplace instructions are unclear, it stresses out our brains and makes us think less effectively.

Brain scans show that confusion triggers our brain's alarm system (the amygdala), which releases stress hormones like cortisol. These hormones slow down the part of our brain that handles complex thinking, problem-solving, and creativity. This is why unclear directions can freeze up decision-making and reduce effectiveness.

Clear leadership does the opposite - it reduces anxiety and increases the willingness for engagement. Brain researcher Dr. David Rock found that certainty is one of five basic social needs that drive human behavior. Essentially, our brains crave clarity.

Therefore, when leaders communicate clearly and openly, they meet this basic need. This frees up mental energy that would otherwise go toward worrying, allowing employees to focus on productive work. People working under clear leadership show better thinking flexibility, improved memory, and longer attention spans.

The business results back this up. Harvard Business Review found that employees with clear communication are 25% more productive and happier at work. Clear leadership creates psychological safety, encouraging people to take initiative and contribute more

Research also shows that organizations focusing on clarity have 37% lower employee turnover and 29% higher innovation compared to those with confusing leadership styles.

Real-World Examples of Leadership Clarity

To further illustrate the power of clarity, here are a few well-known leadership successes.

Apple - Steve Jobs was known for his ability to articulate a clear vision for Apple, focusing on simplicity, innovation, and customer experience. His clear leadership enabled Apple to redefine industries. In product development meetings, Jobs would famously reduce complex product roadmaps to simple, understandable concepts. When launching the iPod, he summarized the revolutionary device's value to "1,000 songs in your pocket" rather than emphasizing technical specifications. He also extended this clarity to Apple's organizational structure, having his leaders assign a single individual for every project task, eliminating confusion about ownership and accountability. Leveraging simplicity, his weekly executive team meetings were structured around a single-page agenda that kept leadership focused on core priorities.

Southwest Airlines - Southwest Airlines' leadership consistently communicated its mission of low-cost, customer-friendly service. Because of that, employees knew exactly how to contribute to that vision, leading to high employee satisfaction and customer loyalty. Former CEO Herb Kelleher reinforced this clarity through consistent messaging about the company's core values. When faced with competitive pressures to add features such as assigned seating or complex fare structures, leadership maintained clarity by rejecting these options because they were contrary to their mission of operational simplicity. Southwest's clarity also extended to their hiring process, where candidates were evaluated primarily on attitude and cultural fit rather than technical skills alone. This clarity of purpose allowed them to maintain profitability for over 30 consecutive years in an industry known for volatility.

Amazon - Founder Jeff Bezos established clear leadership principles that guided decision-making at every level. This clarity helped Amazon scale while maintaining agility and innovative thinking. Bezos emphasized clarity through the company's famous six-page narrative memos, which replaced PowerPoint presentations and forced precise thinking. Amazon's unusual "Working Backwards" process, which begins with writing a press release for a product before development starts, ensured that teams had a crystal-clear understanding of customer value before investing resources. The company's "Day 1" mentality—a constant reminder to maintain the urgency and customer focus of a startup--provided a clear framework for balancing long-term thinking with immediate execution. This clarity enabled Amazon to expand successfully from books to cloud computing to entertainment while maintaining a coherent company identity.

Overcoming Challenges to Implementing Clarity

While clarity is powerful, implementing it is not always easy. Leaders should be on guard for the following obstacles.

Resistance to Change: In some cases, employees and managers who've become accustomed to ambiguity may struggle with new expectations. Their resistance often stems from psychological safety concerns, as unclear or chaotic work environments can paradoxically offer protection from accountability and performance evaluation.

Information Overload: Too much communication can be overwhelming and counterproductive, especially when attempting to reverse previously poor communication. Research shows that cognitive processing capacity decreases by up to 40% when bombarded with an overload of information, creating what neuroscientist Dr. Sophie Leroy called "attention residue". This results in employees struggling to concentrate on new tasks and making more errors.

Misalignment: Different teams or departments of the company may intentionally or unintentionally interpret leadership messages differently, leading to inconsistency and confusion. This "silo effect" occurs when departmental cultures develop their own communication norms and rules on which they choose to operate.

Fear of Making Decisions: Some leaders avoid clarity because it requires taking definitive positions that might later need to be revised. This typically stems from risk aversion and concern about the possible consequences of future revisions.

Complex Organizations: As companies become more complicated, with teams spread across different countries and departments, it gets much harder to maintain clarity and keep everyone on the same page.

Here are a few ways for leaders to address these challenges.

Start with small changes. Rather than overwhelming

everyone with massive change in an attempt to improve clarity, introduce small, measurable changes that foster better clarity. This "small-step clarity approach" focuses on establishing clarity in smaller doses at critical decision points and processes before gradually expanding more broadly across the organization.

Provide training to reinforce the importance of clarity. Train your leaders to identify and eliminate confusing, ambiguous communication patterns while developing more effective messaging. Remember, your leaders are the foundation for better clarity. Invest in them.

Encourage open dialogue. As people feel the freedom to express themselves, leaders have the opportunity to integrate the company vision and values in these interactions and foster alignment. As an added benefit, you will likely find that trust improves as well.

Develop clarity metrics and KPIs. Organizations that measure clarity through employee feedback and communication audits show 34% higher implementation success rates compared to those organizations that have no formal assessments. Remember, if you want to create focus and get results, measure what's important.

Assign clarity champions. Pick people at different levels outside of management to help assist team members in understanding and embracing the clarity initiatives and messages from leadership. Rotate these roles so more employees get involved.

Establish formal feedback loops. Regular surveys that gauge perceived clarity can identify problem areas before they begin to impact performance. Research has shown that quarterly clarity assessments have a direct correlate to sustained productivity improvements

Balance clarity with appropriate autonomy. Giving specific instructions for every tiny aspect of a job can undermine the value employees look for in their position. Leaders must determine where they absolutely must provide detailed direction versus empowering employees or teams in order to produce better outcomes.

Practical Steps for Leaders to Implement Clarity

To bring clarity into an organization, here are several practical ideas that make expectations and direction more transparent for everyone.

Regular town hall meetings serve as powerful platforms where leaders can reinforce the company's vision, values and strategy, helping employees understand how their individual contributions connect and contribute to larger organizational goals.

Storytelling offers another effective tool for leaders seeking to improve clarity. By sharing real examples and narratives that illustrate company objectives and values, leaders can make abstract concepts concrete and memorable. The idea is to use these stories to create emotional connections that help team members internalize what success looks like in practice.

Structured one-on-one meetings between managers and their direct reports is one of the absolute best approaches. This provides the opportunity to develop personal alignment between employees and leadership.These focused conversations provide space to discuss individual goals, address concerns, and clarify expectations in ways that larger meetings cannot accomplish. If you are wondering where you'll find the time to conduct these meetings, ask yourself where you will find the time to deal with the problems that grow from lack of clarity.

Developing training programs specifically focused on

communication and decision-making skills builds greater capabilities for clarity throughout the organization. When everyone learns to communicate with precision and make decisions transparently, clarity becomes embedded in the company culture.

A focus on cross-functional collaboration breaks down departmental silos and promotes a unified message across the organization. When teams work together on projects with a spirit of openness, they develop shared understanding and consistent interpretations of company priorities and approaches.

Create a leadership playbook that defines standardized communication and decision-making frameworks. Not only does this make it easier for managers to succeed as a leader, but it also ensures consistency across the organization. This resource gives managers at all levels clear guidance on how to approach common situations, resulting in predictable and aligned leadership throughout the organization.

Finally, establish an internal mentorship program designed to reinforce leadership values and best practices. As experienced leaders share their knowledge with emerging talent, they pass on not just technical skills but also the communication approaches that foster clarity throughout the organization. Management mastermind groups are also an option.

Final Thoughts: The Lasting Impact of Clear Leadership

Clarity is not a one-time initiative—it is a leadership philosophy. So, be patient and see these efforts as an investment in your people which will pay big dividends.

Organizations that embrace clarity create a workplace where employees are not just workers, but motivated contributors to a shared mission. When leaders commit to transparency, clear expectations, and open communication, they lay the foundation for long-term success.

Knowing the importance of clarity and what you can do

to bring it to your leadership approach is a great start. But it will all come down to this question: "What are you going to do today and tomorrow to put this information into action?"

By implementing these principles, leaders can build an engaged workforce, foster innovation, and drive long-term business success. The power of clarity is transformative—when embraced fully, it creates resilient organizations that thrive in a complex and ever-changing business landscape.

Chapter Ten

The Cost of Having the Wrong People on Your Team

By Ski Swiatkowski

Introduction

Wayne Davis is the owner-founder of Premier Title Insurance Company, a company he'd built with pride from the ground up and was now in its twenty-sixth year. (Note: The actual name of the company and people involved have been changed)

We first met 40 years ago when he was a hungry young real estate agent and I was a rookie mortgage loan officer. He was a great referral source for me in those early days. We celebrated many closings together, and weathered the ups and downs of the housing market.

As I moved on to the management part of my career, we remained friends, but saw each other less frequently. Now, as a management consultant, I found myself sitting across from my old colleague, who was facing a challenge no amount of industry experience had prepared him for.

"Even though this is a tough real estate market we are going through now, we are holding our own financially," Wayne confided in me. "Unfortunately, we've had to trim the staff recently. So, I can understand morale being down. But something else is off with the team. I built this company on relationships and trust, but that culture is slipping away, and I don't know how to get it back."

What unfolded over the next four months revealed a universal truth about leadership: having the right people on your team isn't just about skills and tenure—it's about alignment of attitudes, values, and communication. And sometimes, the most difficult leadership decisions involve people who've been with you since the early days.

The Company Landscape

Premier Title Insurance Company had grown to thirty employees across three branch offices. They built their good reputation by providing service above and beyond that of their competitors. Their clients ranged from individual homebuyers and investors to developers and financial institutions. Their work demanded precision, attention to detail, a strong client service orientation and a good team to meet those demands.

At the center of the current challenges was Alice Winters, the office manager and senior title processor at the company's busiest branch. With 18 years at Premier, Alice had witnessed the company's evolution from a single office to its current size. Her technical knowledge was exceptional—she could process complex title work faster than anyone else and had trained most of the processing staff over the years. Her compensation reflected her contributions; she was the highest-paid employees in the organization other than Wayne.

But Alice had become increasingly vocal in her criticism of Wayne and the company's direction. What had once been occasional complaints had over the years evolved into open disrespect that was poisoning the well for everyone who worked with her and even the other branches.

"I made her an office manager because she knows this business inside and out," Wayne explained during our second meeting. "She's been with me through those difficult start-up years and some very tough real estate markets. So, I feel a sense of loyalty to her. But now it has gotten to the point where she acts like she's doing me a favor by showing up."

He went on to say, "It recently came to my attention that she told a new hire that I don't know how to run a title insurance company. Hey, I may not be the best title company owner. But undermining leadership in front of the staff? That I can't have—no matter how good she is at her job."

The Warning Signs

During my initial assessment phase, I conducted interviews with employees across all three branches. The patterns that emerged painted a troubling picture, particularly at Alice's branch.

Information flowed poorly between her branch and the main office, with knowledge treated as currency rather than a shared resource, making it difficult to serve clients effectively.

Working in her branch had become fear-based. Junior staff members of her staff had to side with her or suffer the consequences. Staff members would make choices based not on what was best for the client or company, but on what would least likely provoke Alice.

The staff had essentially divided into factions—those who aligned with Alice and adopted her negative perspective about company leadership, and those who kept their heads down, increasingly disengaged. Also quite concerning was the divisions between Alice's office and the rest of the organization.

Uncovering the History

Two weeks into my work with Premier, Wayne invited me to lunch at a small restaurant near the main office. Away from the workplace, he revealed details about his history with Alice that shed light on the complex dynamics at play. He shared that Alice had been just his third hire when the company was in its infancy. The early days of Premier Title consisted of just Wayne, his assistant, and a single processor before Alice joined the team. Despite having five years of industry experience that commanded a higher salary than the fledgling company could typically afford, Alice had taken a chance on Wayne's vision.

The depth of their professional relationship extended beyond typical employer-employee bonds. Wayne confided that during particularly difficult financial periods in those early years, Alice had twice deferred portions of her salary to help the company meet payroll obligations. This sacrifice had created a profound sense of indebtedness in Wayne that complicated his current management challenges.

As our conversation progressed, Wayne revealed more recent examples of Alice's problematic behavior. At last month's quarterly company meeting, she had publicly undermined him by announcing to the entire company that Wayne's latest initiative would "fall flat by the summer, just like his other ideas have." Though Wayne had outwardly laughed off the comment and pretended to appreciate the candid feedback, he admitted feeling deeply furious and embarrassed in the moment.

The situation had only deteriorated since then. Alice's disrespect manifested through negative comments on phone calls with personnel from the other branches, disparaging remarks to clients about the company's "outdated policies," visible eye-rolling when Wayne was speaking, and direct criticism of management to clients. Just the previous day, she had told a major real estate referral partner that a delay on their file was due to management's failure to provide the tools they needed.

When I pressed Wayne about why this behavior had been permitted to continue unchecked, he admitted his fear of losing her operational contributions. She processed twice the files of any other employee, was specifically requested by name from clients, and her branch's revenue carried the company through slower periods.

Furthermore, she had built very strong relationships with

several top producing agents at the real estate office across the hall from her branch office. He feared that her relationship was the reason they gave Premier title work. In his mind, if she were gone, Premier would lose that business. And because of market conditions, they needed every title policy premium they could get.

The Root of the Problem

As I dug deeper, it became clear that Alice's negative attitude stemmed from several sources. She felt passed over for the company's operations manager position, watching as Wayne brought in someone from outside to fill the position. She'd also grown comfortable as the indispensable expert—a position threatened by technologies and processes being implemented as well as smart, young new hires who wanted to excel.

Most importantly, her behavior had been tacitly condoned for years. Wayne, grateful for her early commitment to the company and genuinely concerned about production and operational impacts if she left, had allowed her caustic communication style and resistance to change to become entrenched in the culture.

This belief, that technical prowess and connections outweighed behavioral impact, was costing the company dearly, though the expense wasn't showing up on any balance sheet.

The Hidden Costs

Premier was experiencing what Sydney Finkelstein, professor at Tuck School of Business at Dartmouth College calls "expertise trap"—valuing knowledge and business connections over behavior to the detriment of the organization. During one of our private sessions, I asked Wayne if he'd thought about and measured the costs related to this problem. He said he had not given any thought to the cost side of the problem.

"Wayne, whether you are measuring the costs or not, they are still there," I told him. "There's the training expenses for constant new hires at Alice's branch. You have recruitment fees and the value of your time and that of your operations manager in replacing staff. And what about the lost productivity during transition periods as new people come onboard?" I asked.

Beyond these quantifiable expenses lay the deeper cultural costs: collaboration between the other branch offices and Alice's branch was abysmal. This in turn had a huge negative impact on operational productivity. Trust in leadership was eroding company-wide as employees witnessed Alice's disrespect and lack of cooperation continue to be tolerated.

The emotional toll was perhaps the most severe: increased stress and burnout were evident in the faces of staff members. Based on my survey of his personnel, job satisfaction was suffering significantly with 18 of 30 people giving the company a satisfaction grade of 60% or lower. Professional relationships had fractured along loyalty lines, and Wayne's leadership credibility was in a downward spiral.

When I finished, Wayne sat in silence for several minutes. Finally he said, "I've been so focused on what it might cost to lose Alice that I never calculated what it was costing us to keep her."

The Turning Point

The critical moment came during a workshop I facilitated on psychological safety and communication which was held in two separate session, one for the managers and one for their team members. During the team member session, I introduced an exercise where they could anonymously share their experiences with me in writing. These accounts created a powerful mirror reflecting the company's poor communication culture.

The workshop conversation continued around the topics of leadership responsibility, respect, and the difference between candid feedback and destructive criticism. For the first time, team members spoke openly about how the negative communication patterns were affecting their work and wellbeing.

After the workshop, Wayne and I went out for a walk to allow me to review the workshops with him and to share one particular entry from the team member exercise that underlined the cost he was paying. This person wrote: "I used to tell friends that Premier was the best place I'd ever worked. The work mattered, and people cared about doing things right. Now I warn my industry friends not to apply here. I'm told daily that 'Wayne doesn't get it' and 'management is clueless.' I spend more energy navigating office politics than serving clients. I'm exhausted, and I'm updating my resume."

Wayne sat there and stared at me for a while and then began to speak. "I've been complicit in this," he said as we walked. "Every time I let a disrespectful comment slide, I was telling everyone that behavior was acceptable. My sense is that, as a result, others don't respect me as well." At that point, I turned to him and said, "For the sake of the company, are you ready to have a conversation with Alice?" He shook his head affirmatively. "Good," I said. "Let's discuss how this should go."

The Intervention Plan

Based on my assessment, I recommended a three-pronged approach that went beyond just addressing the situation with Alice.

First, we needed to address the individual behaviors directly. Wayne and I role-played a direct conversation with Alice, focusing on specific behaviors rather than character judgments, clearly articulating expectations for professional communication throughout the company, and outlining consequences for continued policy violations.

Second, the organizational structure needed adjustment. The office manager position needed real authority and accountability for maintaining professional standards.

Documenting and sharing institutional knowledge needed to become a priority to reduce dependency on any single employee. Performance metrics needed to include both technical expertise and collaborative behaviors.

Third, a cultural transformation was necessary. This meant establishing regular one-on-one communication between Wayne and his managers, as well as, the managers and their teams, creating channels for constructive feedback about company policies and leadership decisions, and developing recognition systems that celebrated both technical excellence and supportive behaviors.

The Conversation with Alice

Wayne's meeting with Alice was scheduled for a Friday afternoon. We had prepared extensively, anticipating various reactions and planning thoughtful responses. Wayne had documentation of specific incidents, clear expectations for future behavior, and a genuine openness to hearing Alice's perspective.

"How did it go?" I asked when he called me that evening.

"Not well," Wayne admitted. "I started exactly as we practiced—expressing appreciation for her contributions, acknowledging the effects of my often poor communication, and addressing the specific behaviors that could not continue."

Wayne continued, "I offered the path we discussed—continuing in her role with adjusted responsibilities and clear communication expectations for all of us. She laughed and said she'd been carrying this company for years and wasn't about to start asking permission to do her job."

Alice ended the meeting by getting up and walking out of the room without another word. On Monday morning, she submitted her resignation, effective immediately.

The Aftermath and Lessons Learned

At a company meeting held shortly after Alice's resignation,

Wayne addressed his own role in allowing the situation to develop. "I've avoided difficult conversations out of misplaced loyalty and fear," he acknowledged. "That wasn't fair to anyone—not to our team members who deserved a respectful workplace, not to our clients who deserve our best service, and frankly, not to those engaging in the problematic behaviors either. Real respect means believing people can grow and change."

The weeks following Alice's departure were challenging. Some long-time employees initially struggled with the change, and there were inevitable knowledge gaps that needed filling. The branch's processing capacity temporarily decreased as others stepped up to absorb her workload.

But something unexpected also occurred: the atmosphere began to lighten. Ideas for working through the transition began flowing. Collaborative problem-solving increased. People began to take on responsibilities outside of their normal role to ensure better client service.

Three months later, I returned for a follow-up assessment. The transformation was remarkable. The branch that had been under Alice's management was now exceeding previous processing production levels. Most surprisingly, processing times—which Wayne had feared would suffer greatly without Alice's expertise—had improved by 11% through collaborative approaches and knowledge sharing. And, there was no drop in title insurance referrals from the real estate agents served by that branch. Plus, there had not been any turnover in the company since she left. Zero.

During our debriefing at the follow-up assessment, Wayne shared his thoughts about the challenge he had experienced. He told me that he had confused obligation with leadership. He believed he owed Alice unwavering support because of their history together. His epiphany was that he really owed her—and all of the team members—a workplace where people are both valued for their contributions and held accountable for their impact on others.

For years, he told himself keeping Alice was a business decision; that her technical skills outweighed everything else. But it wasn't business; it was avoidance. He was afraid of the confrontation, afraid of looking ungrateful, afraid of short-term pain. In trying to avoid all that, he created something much worse.

Wayne finally understood that having the right people means more than having technically proficient people. It means having people who strengthen rather than weaken your culture. Who communicate with respect even when they disagree. Who remember that how we do things is as important as what we accomplish.

Key Takeaways

Wayne's journey offers several universal leadership lessons.

Having the "right people" on your team transcends skills and experience—it encompasses attitudes and behaviors that either strengthen or weaken your culture. Technical expertise without emotional intelligence and collaborative capacity creates hidden costs that eventually outweigh the benefits. Wayne had to learn that Alice's processing speed and control of potential referral business couldn't compensate for the cultural damage her behavior was causing.

Negative attitudes, especially from influential team members, spread like contagions when left unaddressed. Leaders must have the courage to confront behaviors that undermine team cohesion, regardless of the person's tenure or technical value. The longer these conversations are delayed, the more damage occurs and the harder remediation becomes. Wayne's years of avoiding the issue allowed destructive patterns to become deeply entrenched.

Regular, meaningful two-way communication serves as preventive medicine for organizational problems. This includes creating psychological safety for honest feedback, establishing multiple channels for communication, demonstrating receptiveness to input (especially criticism), and following through on commitments made during discussions. Premier's new communication structures helped prevent minor frustrations from festering into major grievances.

Sometimes, the most loyal leadership decision is parting ways with a long-term employee whose presence has become detrimental to the larger team. This isn't about discarding people—it's about recognizing that some working relationships have run their course despite best efforts on both sides. While losing Alice was difficult, it ultimately freed both her and the company to find better paths forward.

A team's communication culture reflects its leadership's behaviors more than its stated values. Wayne's reluctance to address Alice's communication style effectively endorsed it. When he finally aligned his actions with his espoused values, the organization could begin its transformation.

Conclusion

The Premier Title Insurance Company story illustrates that a single person with a poor attitude—particularly one in a position of influence—can undermine an otherwise healthy organization. It also demonstrates that with the right intervention, courage, and commitment to two-way communication, even entrenched cultural problems can be overcome.

The company continues to thrive, having learned that genuine loyalty to people means creating conditions where everyone can succeed—not protecting behaviors that ultimately harm both the individual and the organization. Their experience reminds us that having the right people, in the right roles, with the right attitudes, isn't just good leadership theory—it's essential business practice with measurable impacts on performance, culture, and sustainability.

About the Authors

Albert B. Blixt The Managing Partner of Dannemiller Tyson Associates, Al has worked in organizational change for more than 25 years. He is a developer and practitioner of the Whole-Scale® approach to bringing about rapid, transformational change for organizations in all sectors, particularly in manufacturing, healthcare, higher education, and non-profit. His work is grounded in the principle that people support what they help to create. He stresses system engagement and tapping the wisdom that is found within each individual. Through uncovering and combining the knowledge and aspirations of the group, new and innovative solutions arise coupled with the energy and commitment to act on them.

Blixt had several careers before consulting, including a high school teacher, a prosecuting attorney, ad agency owner, a business school professor, and an art gallery owner. He is also an auto racing historian, and advocate for persons with developmental disabilities and a volunteer for the Michigan Shakespeare Festival. He brings all of those experiences to his work.

Books Al's has authored or co-authored include: *Whole-Scale Change: Unleashing the Magic in Organizations* and *The Whole-Scale Toolkit, Leading Innovation and Change: A Guide for Chief Student Affairs Officers on Shaping the Future* and *A Guide to Leading a Culture of Strategic Innovation – How College and University Leaders Will Shape the Future.*

Jeffrey Edwards is the founder of The MakeWell Performance Group, where he partners with business leaders to turn strategy into results through a human-centered approach to organizational change. His work is grounded in a simple truth: *business is personal.* Behind every strategic plan are people, and it's the strength of their relationships that determines success.

Drawing from over 25 years in leadership roles across organizations of all sizes, from startups to Fortune 500 companies, Jeffrey equips executives and their teams with tools and mindsets to lead with clarity, confidence, and impact through rapid change and uncertainty.

His coaching and advisory work focuses on leadership presence, team dynamics, and cultural transformation, especially in fast-paced tech and service industries. His specialty is guiding next-generation leaders through the transition into leadership. By uncovering their natural strengths and building authentic presence, he unlocks their ability to lead with purpose and create environments where teams feel safe to speak up, take risks, and perform at their best.

Beyond his client work, Jeffrey is committed to developing future leaders through his involvement with Junior Achievement and the Black Professional Technical Network's Cultivate Program. Based in Ottawa, he is a trusted advisor to those who want more than quick fixes—they want lasting change built on trust, insight, and action..

Dr. Mike Hackney is the founder of ShaydeTree Enterprises, a business consulting and executive coaching company. He did his doctoral work at the University of Southern California in the sustaining change and leadership areas of organizational psychology, and his MBA at the University of Arizona Global Campus.

Mike received his undergrad degree and commission as an Army infantry officer from the University of Alabama. After eight-years on active duty, he began his thirty-year business career in Chicago with PepsiCo, moving to other companies including Sara Lee, ConAgra Brands, and Bar-S Foods—Sigma Alimentos of Mexico.

Mike is a two-time best-selling author/co-author, writing both non-fiction and fiction books. He is also a public speaker and academic researcher. As a general aviation pilot, he contributes to aviation-related publications on flying and aviation safety.

As a manager and business executive, Mike received numerous accolades for turning around under-performing divisions, creating motivated and sustainable cultures, and establishing environments fostering positive operational efficacy and team-member performance. When not working with clients, speaking, or writing, he spends his time with his wife traveling and attending music concerts across the globe.

Robert Grossman is a leadership strategist, executive coach, and founder of Black Diamond Leadership. He helps leaders and teams unlock high performance through emotional mastery, communication, trust, and psychological safety. With more than 25 years of experience advising Fortune 500 companies, growing organizations, and mission-driven nonprofits, Robert designs and facilitates transformational leadership development programs that are practical, interactive, and grounded in real-world results.

Robert's leadership journey began on the slopes—as a ski patroller, team leader, and nationally certified trainer in search and rescue and mass casualty response. These early experiences shaped his deep understanding of teamwork under pressure and the power of purposeful leadership. Before founding Black Diamond Leadership, Robert ran a successful event production company for over two decades, guiding communication and leadership events for clients like Disney, Toyota, Deloitte, and Blue Cross.

A sought-after keynote speaker and frequent podcast guest, Robert is known for his authentic style, compelling stories, and practical tools that help leaders create teams where people feel safe to speak up, take risks, and do their best work.

Arthur "Ski" Swiatkowski is a the founder and CEO of Radical Performance Business Solutions, a coaching, consulting, and training company focused on management-leadership development and performance improvement. His objective in these areas is help clients identify and unleash the God-given potential they have in order to transform their lives, and impact the people they lead and the organizations for which they work.

Ski's interest in performance improvement and leadership that started in his years as a collegiate football player grew into a passion that ultimately fueled his personal success as a manager and executive during his 40 year career in the mortgage industry.

In his personal life, he leveraged his leadership skills to launch, grow and coach high school and youth lacrosse programs in the suburban Philadelphia area.

From his vast experiences, he brings real-world stories and lessons from the boardroom and the playing field which his clients can apply.

A former trainer for the National Association of Mortgage Brokers, he has been a featured speaker at company events and industry trade shows. Ski is also currently a member of the board of directors of *The Scotsman Guide*, one of the premier trade publications for the mortgage industry, and the co-author of *Create the Change You Want to See: Key Strategies to Fuel Your Success*.

COMING SOON:

Becoming Better Business Leaders

VOL. 2

SORDELET ink

Made in the USA
Monee, IL
07 April 2026

47884927R00068